THE REST OF MY LIVES

Elle Nestico

Copyright © 2024 Ellen Nestico

All rights reserved.

ISBN: 979-8-9927760-2-7

Somewhere in time, a
twenty-year-old girl is gazing up at the stars,
wondering what her life will be. To her, I say
~ just wait.

CONTENTS

ACKNOWLEDGMENTS	vii
CHAPTER ONE	1
CHAPTER TWO	16
CHAPTER THREE	32
CHAPTER FOUR	53
CHAPTER FIVE	66
CHAPTER SIX	80
CHAPTER SEVEN	86
CHAPTER EIGHT	91
CHAPTER NINE	101
CHAPTER TEN	110
CHAPTER ELEVEN	118
CHAPTER TWELVE	130
CHAPTER THIRTEEN	138
CHAPTER FOURTEEN	143
CHAPTER FIFTEEN	146
CHAPTER SIXTEEN	156
CHAPTER SEVENTEEN	168
CHAPTER EIGHTEEN	172
CHAPTER NINETEEN	183
CHAPTER TWENTY	202
CHAPTER TWENTY-ONE	210
CHAPTER TWENTY-TWO	215
EPILOGUE	217

ACKNOWLEDGMENTS

Thank you to my crazy, prodigious, wonderful hubbub of a family. You inspire me daily, and without question, I would choose you over and over again.

And to my exceptionally gifted editors, Jess Millman and Lindsey Pastorek of Literary Lift Editing, my uber-talented artist, Rachel Sierra, and my best friends turned beta readers. Your creativity, expertise, love, and support have been everything.

CHAPTER ONE

2022
Emi

"There you are. I've been waiting for you."

He ran a forefinger down her nose as sunbeams danced between the leaves and over his boyish smirk. They lay on a soft bed of white down, under a canopy of evergreens, shielded by branches that stretched high to the morning sun. He wrapped his hands around her waist and slid her into the little spoon position, his skin warm like smoldering embers in the early spring chill.

"Sorry, I'm awake now." She gave a raspy yawn, smiling lazily from inside his tattooed arms.

"It's okay. You know I'd wait forever," he whispered.

She sighed, safe and content, while a bluebird sang happily from somewhere deep in the woods.

Emi jerked as the chimes of her smartphone dashed her sleep. Pulling off her satin eye mask and sliding it over a chocolate bird's nest of hair, she rolled over to find the other side of the bed cold and empty. Déjà vu rushed through her veins and tingled up her spine, and she huffed with disappointment at the morning that had come too soon.

Emi slid defiantly under her sheets, closed her eyes, and tried to will herself back to her dream. But no matter how much she racked her brain, she couldn't quite remember who she had been tangled up so intimately with just a moment before. Her stomach lurched with an unsettling flash of espresso eyes staring back at her, piercing and beautiful, but definitely not her husband's.

Retracing her steps in the dim place between asleep and awake, she was about to slip through the door that would take her back when her phone alarm screamed again. Emi let out a defeated sigh and prepared herself for another chaotic morning of getting three kids dressed, fed, and off to school.

She swung her legs over the side of the bed and sat up. Emi's eyes rested on a construction paper card with *mamma* crudely sprawled across the front in purple crayon, waiting patiently on her dresser, accompanied by a dozen red roses. Next to them, a latte steamed in her favorite mug.

Fuck me.

It's my fortieth birthday.

"Oh my God, Mom, this is so exciting!"

Violet slammed the car door, strawberry blond hair falling out of her neon-pink claw clip. Her eyes, the same color as her father's, shone like polished amber. She leaned close to the passenger side mirror to slather on pink lip oil and make kissy faces at herself while Emi climbed out of her SUV.

"I've always wanted you to pick me up in the middle of the day for no reason. And you even got me before algebra!"

"I thought we could use a mommy-daughter day. Let's start with an iced latte," Emi said with a smile.

"Dad is going to freak. You know how he is about school."

"I already talked to him about it," she lied. "Don't worry, it's my birthday. He can't get mad."

As she and Vi walked arm in arm through the large glass doors of the mall, her designer cross-body bag thumping against her hip with each step, Emi knew busting her daughter out of school early had been a good call. She was pleased to feel Vi relax, even for a few hours. These blissful moments between them were few and far between, and though she was terrified of the hormonal storm that seemed to be perpetually swirling through her daughter, she was determined to enjoy every second of softness.

"Do I have a budget?" Vi asked, fingers crossed.

"Not really. Let's just be reasonable. We can grab a late lunch in a bit, and then . . ."

Emi stammered and blinked hard as she cut her sentence short. A good-looking middle-aged man was walking behind Violet, out of one store and into another. There was something familiar about his olive complexion and the shape of his brow. A part of Emi that had long been curled up tightly and tucked away stirred in its slumber.

"Uh, hello?" Vi chuckled as she waved a hand in front of Emi's eyes. "Mom, you look like you saw a ghost!"

"What? Oh." Emi gave an awkward laugh as she came to. "I just, um. I thought I recognized that man for a second. He reminds me of someone, maybe. But I can't remember who."

"What man?" Violet turned around, but it was too late. He was gone.

"Oh, nobody. I don't know. He probably just looks like someone I went to school with or something. Don't worry about it." Emi took a deep breath and rubbed away the goosebumps spread over her arms.

"Alright, boomer, our Starby's is waiting." Vi grabbed her hand and pulled Emi and her wallet toward the bright green letters of the coffee shop.

"I'm a millennial."

"Trust me, Mom, we can tell."

Two and a half hours of watching her daughter violate her credit card while pretending to care about the entwined gossip of Vi's hundred friends ticked slowly by before Emi could finally throw herself into a dining chair in one of the mall's dim restaurants. Violet pursed her lips as she scrolled through her phone and twirled her golden hair mindlessly. As Emi eyed her beautiful, yet terrifying firstborn, she bemusedly contemplated the identifying traits of Stockholm syndrome.

"And oh my God, I can't wait to wear my new Lulu to school tomorrow. Ugh, I need to do a haul." Her face dropped, and she scowled across the table. "Mom?"

"Oh, yeah, that'll be great, super cute." Emi pulled her menu over her face in an attempt to escape. For an extroverted introvert, teenaging for extended periods, even with her own child, was tiresome.

Relief came in the form of a waiter dressed in all black, and Emi mouthed a 'thank God' from her hiding place.

"Hello, ladies. May I start you with a drink?"

"Mom, can I get a mocktail? I'll have the Spicy Watermelon Mint Agua Fresca, please," Vi said in her best adult voice, trying very hard to be nonchalant. Emi stifled a smile as it occurred to her that the world may not be ready for her bougie daughter. In true Vi fashion, even her drink orders were complicated.

"That sounds delicious. I think I'll have the same. Thank you," Emi said politely.

As she handed their menus to the waiter, her eyes fell on his nametag.

Jesse

Emi's stomach flipped with recognition, and goosebumps freckled her once more. The mystery man she had seen earlier in the mall looked just like Jesse.

Jesse Amato.

After dropping Vi off at home and retrieving her second extra-large iced latte for the day, Emi had a busy afternoon of errands. She popped into the dry cleaner's to pick up Josh's work suits, the grocery store for little Liam's peewee soccer snacks, and the vet for their golden retriever's heartworm medicine. As she pulled into the parking lot of the baseball clinic where Jack, her oldest son, was practicing, suddenly she was hyper aware of her car rattling with bass.

I wonder if any other suburban sports moms listen to nineties gangster rap, or is it just me?

Parents stood around the batting cages; some were waiting awkwardly by themselves, pretending to be captivated by their phones, while others made forced small talk near the cubbies. Emi straightened her spine and strutted to her spot, trying not to compare her leggings and lifestyle sneakers to the business attire everyone else prescribed to.

The coach called for the kids to leave their stations and meet him on the gym floor.

"Alright, guys, everybody did great today. I'm so excited about the spring season. Keep practicing. Okay, bring it in. 'Reds' on three. Jack, sound it off."

The huddle of boys stuck their hands together in the air.

"One, two, three," Jack yelled.

"Reds," the group screamed in unison, bringing their hands down and then up again. They broke, and all turned to find their parents at once. Jack searched the room for his mom. His face softened as their eyes connected, and he playfully stuck his tongue out at her, his freckles scrunching on his cheeks.

"Wait, honey, where's your hat?" Emi asked on the way to the car. Jack stopped to rifle through his enormous sports bag.

"Not again," he groaned and ran back inside.

Emi leaned against the hood of her SUV and breathed in the beautiful spring sunshine that she had longed for all winter. As her skin took in the warm air, something nearby caught her eye.

A bluebird chirped at her from a small tree, and she smiled back at it.

Where is that boy? she wondered, checking her watch. As her boredom hardened into concern, Emi gave up and walked back to the building, intent on finding out what was holding Jack up.

With her bright pink nails tightly grasping the door handle, she was just about to pull when the door itself came flying at her, and the glass smacked her hard on the forehead.

"Ow! Fuck!"

Emi's vision blackened with pain, and she instinctively covered her face, wobbling backward. She stumbled, and her feet tripped over each other. With nothing to catch herself on, she hurled toward the sidewalk.

As if by divine intervention, before slamming into the concrete, two large hands wrapped around her waist. Someone with strength plucked her body from the air and pulled her in tightly. Cradled against a brawny chest, Emi registered a familiar scent of pine, and her brain searched for the memory.

"Oh my God, I am so sorry," a deep voice said, horrified. "Are you okay?"

He placed her on her feet but kept his arms protectively around her as she struggled to collect herself.

God, how many people saw that? So embarrassing.

"I'm okay. Really, thanks," she said, still behind her hands. Her forehead was raw and throbbing, but inside, Emi cringed at her vanity; she was more worried about her pretty face.

"I am so sorry, ma'am."

"Ma'am?" Emi squawked. That was the final straw. "You can bash my head in, mister, but you absolutely cannot call me 'ma'am.'"

He chuckled. "Yes, of course. I'm sorry."

Wincing, she removed her hands and batted her lashes open, squinting into the sun. Her vision swirled as the light behind him blacked out his facial features.

"Emi? Emi Klein?"

I know that voice . . .

Emi's heart pulled away from its arteries, dropped out of her chest cavity, and fell with a splat onto the ground right where she stood.

Holy. Shit.

"Holy shit," she said. Suddenly, everything around her melted away. In the full three seconds it took her pupils to dilate, a montage of whispers and snapshots of his fingers tracing her body rushed the synapses of her brain.

He scooped her up into a hug inside his large, warm arms, and Emi forgot all about her head. Everything escaped her: the world around them, who she was, and what she had been doing.

I must be dreaming.

"Jesse Amato?"

"I thought that was you! Emi Klein, more beautiful than ever," he said with a grin. "Even with a big ole bump on your head." Heat rushed to her cheeks as he gently touched her bruised forehead. Emi melted as his fingertips felt so familiar and sincere, like a whisper from a previous life.

"Yeah, well. Wow. You look great, too. I guess time has been good to us," she said.

Jesse did look good. He was rested and tan, still lean and sculpted. He wore fitted sweatpants and a baseball hat, his tribal tattoos running down from the sleeves of his snug tee. Suddenly, Emi became very aware of the everything-flavored bagel she had stuffed in her mouth an hour before.

Please don't let me have anything in my teeth, she thought as she covertly ran her tongue across the inside of her mouth.

"I really got you good there," Jesse said, flashing her a broad and apologetic smile. "We have to stop meeting like this. I'm starting to think it's me."

"This time it was," Emi laughed, rubbing her head. "What are you doing here, Jesse? Do you live here? Is one of your kids at the clinic?" she asked, scanning the parking lot, expecting an annoyingly beautiful, super-model-esque wife to step out of a car.

He studied her as he took his time answering. "My sister lives in Aspinwall, just down the road. She moved here years ago with her ex. And my nephew had baseball practice, so I'm picking him up to give her a break and take him off her hands for the day." Emi couldn't help but watch his perfect lips move smoothly over his words.

"No kids of my own, though. Single." Jesse held up a ringless left hand. "I mean, I've had girlfriends, a lot of girlfriends," he stammered, "but you know, nothing has panned out. Uh, not yet, I mean."

His over-explanation was lost on her. All Emi heard was that he was single, but with her wave of relief came a flood of shame.

I'm married. What do I care?

"Do you live close by?" she asked.

"Nah. I live in Aspen, Colorado. But I come back from time to time. You know, to check up on the fam. What about you?"

She trembled slightly as she peered into his eyes, still so dark brown she couldn't see his pupils. It made her nervous that they also seemed transfixed by hers.

"Mom, are you okay?" Jack's concerned voice yanked her from the current she had ridden away on.

Emi twisted around to discover her son standing behind her, hat on his head, looking suspiciously from her to Jesse.

"Oh, yeah, honey. It's just a bump." She stepped back, dulling the glimmer she hoped her son hadn't noticed in her eyes.

"Hey there," Jesse said kindly. "I'm an old friend of your mom's."

"This is my son, Jack. Jack, this is Jesse."

"'Sup." Jack nodded curtly and shot him a look. It wasn't like him to be cold to anyone, especially adults. "Can we go now?"

Can he tell this 'friend' is different from the others? I have to get Jack out of here.

"Well, it was so nice to see you," Emi said briskly.

"Oh, sure. I don't want to keep you," Jesse blurted. "It was great to see you, too. Really great." She smiled and turned away before he could say anything else to make her want to stay on that sidewalk forever.

Emi forced one foot in front of the other until she opened her driver's side door. She could feel Jesse's eyes on her back the whole way, and when she glanced up for one final look, he was still standing right where she had left him. Emi flushed and waved awkwardly, ever cognizant of her outward appearance.

Just a totally platonic run-in with an old friend. Be normal, Emi, be normal.

But nothing about their interaction felt platonic. Her heart broke to leave him there. It felt wrong and unnatural, like her ship was sailing away from the lighthouse, not toward it.

This was how it had always been with Jesse. The intensity of her emotions, even now, was freaking her out. They were still razor-sharp years later.

And yet, she smirked, *I'm still the one running away.*

As her car pulled out of the parking lot, Emi couldn't bear to acknowledge the trapdoor that had suddenly appeared in her life again. Jesse was her Achilles heel, and she knew how easily she could get tripped up and fall through it once more.

Nope. Everything is fine. Totally fine. Nothing to see here.

If she allowed herself to peek through the hatch, she would find that nothing good could come from seeing Jesse Amato again. And though she didn't want to admit it, Emi knew she would never be the same.

Emi rounded a corner onto their road, a serene street lined with large maple trees and sprawling homes buttressed by expansive lots. She pulled up to a big, cream-colored brick house with crisp black shutters and oversized French front doors.

The SUV squeezed into the garage, making sure not to run over the plethora of sports gear that spilled into the third car bay. Jack flopped out of his seat and bounded up the garage stairs, his baseball bag slung over one shoulder, and crashed through the door leading into the house.

What was once a spacious mud room was now filled to the brim with kid paraphernalia. Thick built-ins with coats and backpacks on every hook wrapped around the entryway. Jack kicked off his sneakers and threw them aimlessly to one side as Emi followed her son through the house, pausing briefly to pick up his dirty shoes and put them away with a huff.

"Jack! There is literally a bin for your dirty sneakers right next to the door . . ." She trailed off, realizing she was probably wasting her breath. But as Emi turned the corner, she jumped in shock.

"Surprise! Happy Birthday!"

Her brain jammed as it processed the people standing in front of her.

Those she loved most in this life were stuffed in her kitchen, beaming with excitement. Her three beautiful kids—Violet, Jack, and Liam—her loving husband, Josh; her sister, Rose; and her oldest friend, Fae, with her two daughters. She almost had to pinch herself.

"You guys." She shrugged. "I said I didn't want a party."

"We know," Josh said, giving her his trademark easy laugh as he made his way over. "It's not a party, just cake and family."

If this is forty, I'm all in.

Josh gave her a loving squeeze, a kiss on the cheek, and took her purse. He donned his Pittsburgh Steelers Super Bowl Champs apron and a 'just enjoy it' look. He was a few years older than Emi and had just begun to accumulate some slight wrinkling around his eyes when he smiled. Though he was always cute, aging somehow made him more attractive.

Josh sat her down at the table while Violet carried over a large birthday cake. The wet, black nose of Maddie, the dog, was in hot pursuit.

"Happy Birthday, dear Mamma, happy birthday to you!"

"Blow out the candles, Zia!" Zoe, Fae's oldest daughter, squealed, candle flames dancing in her big green eyes.

"Don't worry, Ma. These aren't the candles you got Dad on his fortieth." Jack laughed. "Remember? You almost lit the house on fire."

"That was an accident," Emi exclaimed. "I thought they were just regular candles. Until they started sparkling everywhere."

Rose snickered. "Josh had to dump water on it and stuff it in the grill to put it out."

"Am I ever going to live that down?"

"Don't forget to make a wish, Mamma!" Liam had climbed up into her lap and clasped his pudgy, five-year-old hands in delight.

Emi closed her eyes and blew out the lopsided four and zero candles the kids had smashed into the cake. Then Josh whisked it away to the marble island where he began divvying up slices to the children-turned-angry mob, each one demanding their dessert. Sauvignon Blanc glugged out of a blue bottle as Rose poured herself, Fae, and Emi all large glasses.

"Thanks for coming, girls," Emi said as she raised her glass in a cheers.

"Of course," Rose said. "It's not every day my baby sister turns forty. God, you're getting old."

"Yeah—and speaking of old. Holy shit, you guys," Emi said more quietly. "You will never guess who I ran into today."

Rose wrinkled her nose. "Ew, I hope it wasn't Sandra. I swear, she's obsessed with me."

"Just take it as a compliment." Fae laughed. "I would love to have someone obsessed with me at this point."

"It's the sex. I'm hard to forget."

"Oh my God, gross. Rose, no." Emi shook her head emphatically. "I ran into Jesse Amato," she said, glancing over her shoulder. The girls stared at her, Rose in confusion but Fae in disbelief.

"Jesus, help us," Fae sighed. "Did he see you?"

"Yeah, I talked to him."

Rose caught the serious but silent look Emi and Fae exchanged across the table. "Remind me who that is again?"

"He's just some kid from twenty years ago," Emi said, purposefully downplaying his significance.

"Oh, yeah. You mean that guy you had a crush on in college?" Rose flashed a teasing smirk. "It's all coming back to me. Weren't you blackout drunk and ran away without telling anyone?"

"Uh, yeah, thanks for the recap. I still maintain that was Fae's fault. I have never humiliated myself so much in my entire life. If I had just gone home with Dante Apreal, like I was supposed to that night, I could have saved myself a lot of grief."

"Dante Apreal? Fae did you a favor," Rose said with a glint in her eye as she took a sip of her wine.

Fae grinned and gave a mocking little bow. "I'm here to serve."

"Anyway, I never saw Jesse again after that. And there he was, two decades later, at Jack's baseball clinic. Look." Emi pointed to her forehead. "He accosted me with the door."

Fae shot her another look.

"It was an accident. Anyway, that's not the weirdest part. Earlier, when Vi and I were shopping, I could have sworn I saw Jesse in a store. It wasn't him, but what are the odds I bump into him two hours later?"

Fae's face dropped from accusatory to concerned.

"Didn't you say he looked just like Channing Tatum?" Rose asked.

"Yeah. He still does."

Fae cleared her throat in annoyance, and they all knew to move on.

"How's the new house coming?" Rose asked her.

"Pretty well," Fae answered. "The girls like it. And it helps a lot that my mom is just around the corner." She twisted her bright blond hair around one finger. It was a tell Emi and Rose, after years of growing up together, knew well. They shared a look of concern.

Josh stopped by just long enough to deliver cake before tiptoeing away to play with the kids.

"I know you have an attorney already," Rose said, "but you know I'm always here for advice if you need it."

"Thanks, Rosie. I know. I wouldn't have been able to leave and start over without you guys. Especially you, Em. Driving all the way to Philly in the middle of the night to pack me and the girls up meant more than you'll ever know."

"Fae, that's what family is for. You know you're more than a friend to us. We're always here for you."

Fae's chin wiggled.

"Right now, I'm just trusting what the universe puts in front of me and hoping that I'm following its plan. And Tyler just isn't a part of it anymore."

"Well, I don't know about all that 'universe has a plan' bullshit." Rose huffed. "But you definitely deserve to be happy."

"What, you don't believe in destiny?" Fae asked.

"No. I don't. I think life is what we decide to make of it. Everything is a consequence of our choices. Good or bad. And when we die, that's it, we're just dead. No afterlife, purpose, or plan. Destiny is a concept we invented to make ourselves feel better when shit goes wrong."

"Rosie has always been a skeptic, Fae, you know that."

"I wouldn't say a 'skeptic' per se. I'm a realist. I don't believe in God or the universe being something other than a big, black void of floating rocks and gas. I don't believe in psychics or tarot cards or gemstones or any of that crap. But listen, you're entitled to your own opinions. Even if they are dumb."

"Rosie, you are a dagger in my heart," Fae exclaimed. Her voice was lighthearted, but she looked a bit gobsmacked at her skepticism. "Who hurt you, girl?"

"I think it's fun," Emi said. "We run the spiritual spectrum. Fae, you're a full-hearted, devout believer in all things spiritual. Rosie, you're a cynic and a true non-believer."

"Where does that put you, then?" Rose asked Emi.

"Somewhere in the middle, I guess."

Fae put her wine glass down with a decisive clink.

"You do know your sister's psychic, right?"

Rose cocked a disbelieving eyebrow.

"Don't give me that face. She's had clairvoyant dreams ever since we were little, you know that. Emi's dreamt of all sorts of things that have come true. Haven't you, Em?"

"I mean, yeah. I guess some of them have. But I don't know about the 'clairvoyant' part. I don't see dead people or anything."

"My psychic says everyone's gifts are different. You get déjà vu all the time, and you're definitely pre-cognitive. Remember when you told me that you had a vision of us at my dad's funeral?"

"Wow, we were so little when that happened. I can't believe you remember that. It's been what, thirty years?"

"It must've been because we were only seven or eight when you told me you saw us all dressed in black, holding hands on the church pew."

"Oh, right. I didn't understand the context because I had never been to a funeral before. It's weird, but I can still see that vision, just as clear in my mind like I had it yesterday."

Rose squinted. "But, like, are you actually remembering a vision, or is it just a memory of us from the funeral?"

"I don't know."

Fae huffed. "What about when you dreamt of Josh's sister a few nights before we ran into him on the street, and you two started dating? And you said Zoe came to you in a dream before I even knew I was pregnant, and you told me what she'd look like. You said she was a girl with green eyes. Like, how many people have green eyes?"

Rose chuckled at them both. "Well, little sister, maybe you do have 'the gift,'" she said with a sarcastic wink. "I think it sounds lucrative. What do I need to do to get you in a dream with the winning lottery numbers? I'd love an early retirement."

"Haha, very funny," Emi answered with a snark.

"Lotto or not, your intuition is always on point. I think it is about time you start to trust it and pay attention to this gift of yours," Fae said.

"I have a big surprise for you," Josh whispered as he ushered Emi into the bedroom and shut the door behind him. "Is everyone asleep?"

"Yes, the boys are. And Vi's locked up in her room on FaceTime with her boyfriend, so we won't be seeing her until tomorrow."

His eyes gleamed impishly as he held up a bag of brightly colored THC-infused gummy bears.

Emi clapped her hands like a child. "You'd better lock that door."

Josh hopped on one foot from the door to the bed while kicking off his pants with the excitement of an adolescent boy. His clothes could have been on fire, he got them off so fast. Emi laughed at him as she grabbed the gummy bears, popped one in her mouth, and climbed onto the bed. Adrenaline rushed warmly through her body as her excitement grew.

"Alexa, play our 'sexy time' playlist," he commanded, and he slowly crawled over the comforter to his wife, stalking her like a lion eyeing his dinner. But taking one look at the playful expression in his eyes, Emi laughed again.

He kissed her lustfully, then pulled her bra off and tossed it over his shoulder, and they held each other close.

"Happy Birthday," Josh said.

He flipped her on her back, and she closed her eyes as they melted into each other. Emi's weed gummy kicked in, and she felt herself smile warmly as love, time, and space began its hurricane swirl all around them.

Wrapped up cozily in Josh's arms, Emi dozed peacefully. The TV flickered in the dark as a documentary about Einstein and his theory of relativity droned from across the room. Her eyelids grew heavier and heavier, and fighting them was futile.

"That is so cool," Josh said under his breath, absorbed by the show. "Can you imagine if one day we could go back in time?"

Emi smiled softly in acknowledgment. In her subconscious, she watched her feet tiptoe down a luminary-lit stone path, treading peacefully toward that place between sleep and awake. Her mind wandered into the dark, and she floated out of her body to watch from above.

Peering down on herself and Josh, snuggled up tightly in their bed, warmed Emi's heart. She looked so happy in his embrace. As Emi drew closer and closer to her own smile, losing sight of everything else, she glanced down to admire the dark ink that swirled across her husband's branded arms. They blended organically with the blanket of leaves and wildflowers that pillowed beneath while a purple silhouette of darkened woods surrounded them, the stars close enough to touch.

But before Emi's brain could fully comprehend what it was watching, the stars flickered in and out, and she lay in cool sheets again, asleep within the walls of her cozy bedroom.

A lucid unease spread through her. *Josh doesn't have tattoos.*

CHAPTER TWO

The party pedaler bus stopped on a busy downtown street, bumping early two-thousands rap while cars and buses whooshed past. Eight gorgeous millennial moms, complete with medi-spa treatments and expensive athletic wear, finished their White Claws and giggled off their pedal stools. They strode into the first bar on the pub crawl, two at a time, arm in arm, as if they owned the place.

Emi was still singing the chorus of Nelly's "Country Grammar" as she removed her oversized sunglasses and bopped her way to the front of the sleepy bar.

"Eight lemon drops, please," she said with an easy laugh as she leaned over to get the bartender's attention. Seemingly amused by the bougie group that had just invaded his pub, he obliged with a smile.

"Thanks for the best birthday, ladies," Emi said, holding up her drink to her friends. "I love you guys so much!"

They broke out into a wave of happy birthday cheers.

"And special thanks to Fae," Emi added, "for conspiring with my husband and planning it all under my nose, since God knows she never could keep a secret from me to save her life."

"Oh, that's right," Lauren, one of Emi's closest mom friends, said as she turned to Fae. "Emi mentioned you've been friends since middle school."

"Elementary school. I moved onto her block right before second grade." Fae smiled. "We were best friends from the moment she knocked on my door and asked me to join her Cat Club."

Emi was in awe. "I totally forgot about the Cat Club! I'm pretty sure all we did was draw pictures of cats."

"How could I say no to that? Plus, you were so cute with your little brown pigtails. Anyway, we moved to Squirrel Hill when my dad was diagnosed with cancer so we could be closer to the university hospital. When he died, my mom struggled with depression, so I spent a lot of time at Emi's house after school and on weekends—when they weren't traveling around the world, of course. Her family kind of took me in."

"That's so sweet," Lauren said. "And then you went to the University of Pittsburgh together?"

"We were Semple Street's reigning beer pong champs two years in a row. Those SAE boys didn't know what hit them," Emi added with a laugh. "Ah, the good old days."

The conversation splintered into groups of two or three. Topics ranged from everyone else's debaucherous college stories to favorite true crime documentaries to the difference between Botox and Daxxify before circling back to Fae.

"So, when did you move back home?"

"Well"—Fae cleared her throat—"it's been maybe four months now. My husband and I just couldn't make it work. Nothing super scandalous happened. We just grew apart. We had been for years, probably ever since our wedding day. Something changed in me when I turned forty; I finally found the courage to leave."

"I completely get it. I'm on my second marriage. It gets easier, I promise. When did you—"

Emi cut in, saving Fae from the hot seat, knowing there was more to this story than she could or would tell.

"You know what the worst part about marriage is? Fucking dinner," she quipped. "It never ends. It's like, Jesus, didn't I just do that yesterday? But then four o'clock smacks me in the face, and I'm like, shit, I have to do that today, too?" And they were off again in their own little clusters of chitchat.

"Oh my God, totally." Lauren laughed. "But if 'what are we eating' is my biggest problem, I guess it's okay."

Emi nodded. "I'm so grateful that Josh and I are financially secure enough for me to stay home and focus on the kids. I know what a privilege that is. But do you ever miss doing things for yourself?"

"Like what, honey?"

"Not like spa treatments and yoga class or ladies' night. But, like, I think I miss working. I used to be a writer, and I loved it."

Lauren scoffed. "You couldn't pay me to go back to work. My kids are enough for me to handle. Parent-teacher conferences, Girl Scouts, ballet. If something has to fall by the wayside, it won't be them."

Emi smiled, but she could feel it didn't reach her eyes. She took a large gulp of her mojito as panic grew from her gut and sprang into her chest.

"Yeah," she said. "You're right."

But no—no, she's not. Maybe being a stay-at-home mom works for Lauren, but it's not working for me. At least, not anymore.

Does loving my family mean I can't have anything for myself? Will I ever get to be my own person again?

Emi excused herself from the table before she fell further down the rabbit hole. After having navigated through three sticky bouts of postpartum, she could spot an intrusive thought a mile away and reminded herself to breathe.

"What's up?" Fae gave her a knowing look as she slid onto a barstool beside her.

"Nothing." But Emi didn't even have to meet her eyes to know she wasn't buying it. "Do you ever miss the 'old' us? Like, before husbands and kids. You know, when we were young and spontaneous."

"Spontaneous, like when we drove six hours to the beach at two in the morning after binge drinking all night just to watch the sunrise?"

They laughed in fond memory of that night. Fae, smiling dreamily, held up a finger and ordered them two more drinks.

"Yeah, I do. But we are still the same old us, Em. We just have to schedule our shenanigans now." She chuckled. "But I know you better than that. What's really going on?"

"I've been thinking." Emi shot her eyes to the floor.

"Yeees," Fae coaxed, drawing out her vowels. "Thinking about?"

Emi cleared her throat and took in a deep breath.

"I've been finding myself thinking about"—she swallowed a large lump and then blurted—"Jesse."

"Aha! I knew it!" Emi rolled her eyes at Fae's vindication. "Is that where all of this is coming from?"

"Honestly, maybe. Ever since I saw him the other day, I've been thinking about my life. Like, where I am and where I thought I'd be. And it's fine, things are great. Josh is great, and we're happy. But I guess I just have been wondering, like, whatever happened to that girl I used to be? You know, the girl with all the dreams."

"Yeah, I know. I wondered that about myself for a long time. That's one of the reasons why I left Tyler. But you're still that girl, Emi. I see her all the time."

"That's it, though. I don't have enough time to be her."

Taking a long drink from her straw, Fae twisted around on the stool, giving Emi her complete and undivided attention.

"Okay, in the last six weeks, I have had a total of three days when I wasn't taking care of a sick child. First, it was the flu; then Liam got hand, foot, and mouth from some kid in his class; and then it was that awful stomach bug that was going around. Everyone was throwing up at four in the morning, and of course, I was the only one to deal with it because Josh was in Phoenix on a work trip.

Someone has been home from school every fucking day. I have no personal space. Liam can't go two minutes without asking me a question. He sticks his little fingers under the bathroom door when I pee. And even though Vi's in her sleep-all-day stage, I can feel her hormonal poltergeist energy seeping through the walls. I'm, like, legitimately scared of her because I don't know which one of her personalities will walk into the room. And then there's the dog, errands, and house. The other day, I burst into tears when Josh didn't empty the dishwasher when I asked him to because it was just one more thing I had to do. At some point, I honestly wanted to jump out of a window. I mean, not really, but you know.

I love my family so much." She leaned in as if she were about to say something horrible. "But, like, sometimes I fantasize about getting sick enough to stay in the hospital where someone else can take care of me for a change. Not like, respirator-sick. But if I could end up in quarantine for a week just for observation, that would be ideal."

Fae burst out laughing. "Oh my God, that sounds amazing! I secretly fantasize about faking my own kidnapping and spending a week in Mexico. I'd come back, of course, but not before I finished reading my book on the beach. I would have to explain my tan to the authorities, though," she said thoughtfully.

"Seriously, Fae, I do wonder sometimes what life would be like without my family. Is that terrible?"

Fae shook her head. "No, I get it. I think every parent does from time to time. And you've always been so independent. You're too intelligent to be stuck at home."

"Writing used to be my whole identity. I wanted to be an author, but now I don't have enough energy to string three sentences together much less write a novel. And I was cocky and free-spirited. I wanted to travel— and not how Josh wants to. Don't get me wrong, I love a good five-star resort. But I wanted to backpack through Europe and really explore the world through other people's eyes. I wanted to eat street food and learn about other cultures. Luxury is great, but there's no danger in Michelin stars, and I wanted adventure.

And now? I can't tell you who I am besides Mrs. Felice. I'm Josh's wife and Vi, Jack, and Liam's mom. I'm boring.

I would never give up what I have. My family is everything; that's not in question. I just want all the other stuff, too. I guess I want it all."

"First of all, you are anything but boring. And I totally understand what you're saying, but how does this circle back to Jesse? Is it because he's single and unencumbered?"

Emi nodded. "Yeah, probably."

"Give me your phone." Fae outstretched her palm, and Emi reflexively handed it over.

"Wait, why? Oh my God, Fae, don't you *dare* do what I think you're doing."

"What? I'm just looking him up. How many 'Jesse Amato's' could there be?" She began banging away on the tiny keyboard before Emi could protest or snatch it away.

"I don't think that's a good—"

"Here he is! Oh, shit."

"What? Is it bad?"

Frowning, Fae slid the phone back to Emi, who hesitated before picking it up. Her stomach flipped with nervous excitement at Jesse's dark eyes staring back at her through the screen.

"It's a total disaster," Fae said, more to herself than to Emi. "He's hot, single, and independently wealthy. He's a forty-year-old finance-bro fuck boy. God, you know I still hate him, right?"

"To be fair, he didn't really do anything to me."

"Exactly. That's what I hate about him." She took a large gulp of her drink. "He's a pussy. He hurt your feelings and embarrassed you. Which, as any adequate best friend would find, is more than enough for me to despise him forever." Fae huffed indignantly and crossed her arms. "Do you know how many bathroom stalls I wrote his number in after all of that?"

"What? Fae!"

"I hope every girl in the city prank-called him. I know I sure did," she boasted. "Serves him right."

The grin slid off Emi's face when she looked down at her phone again. The indented blue button glared back at her, and she retched.

Holy shit.

"What the fuck? You sent him a friend request? This is my phone, Fae. He's going to think I did it!"

Emi laughed maniacally out of panic, but Fae just looked at her.

"Why would you do that if you hate him so much?"

"Because, Emi," Fae sighed. "Forty is too old for wishes and regrets."

It was almost one a.m. when Emi stumbled through the bedroom door as quietly as possible. In her drunken haze, she still remembered not to wake up the kids.

Josh, startled, looked up from the bed, where he had been watching TV, waiting for her. They locked eyes, and he snickered at her inebriated state.

"I take it you had fun, then?"

Emi nodded with an inebriated grin, pulled off her sneakers, and made her way to the bathroom.

"So much fun," she mumbled around the toothbrush buzzing in her mouth. She had channeled old Emi and let herself be both spontaneous and a little wild that night, leaving her spirits renewed.

"I recorded SNL for you. The weekend update was good tonight. I know Michael Che is your favorite." He picked up the remote to rewind it for her, but Emi had other plans.

She sauntered over and stood right in front of him. Josh looked up as she gripped her T-shirt and yanked it up and over her head. He tossed the remote aside and pulled Emi on top of him with a large grin.

"I love it when you come home from ladies' night."

Her hands ran up and down his back, the two of them moving seamlessly together in a lustful mess of skin and sex. He rolled her over, and she climbed on top of him, and he reached up to put his hands on her breasts. The heat from their bodies steamed in the night, and moonbeams that streamed between the trees above lit his face.

Emi arched her back and looked down at him. His eyes glazed with pleasure, Jesse looked up and smiled.

Emi's eyes shot open wide, and she looked around, terrified. The clock read 6:16 a.m., and she felt someone lying next to her in the predawn, cocooned in the covers. Almost too afraid to move, she mustered the courage to sit up and peer over the blankets at his face. Only then did Emi breathe a sigh of relief. Josh slumbered soundly in their bed, his CPAP machine gently whirring, happy and warm.

It was a dream, just a dream.

But though she reassured herself it wasn't real, Emi brought a hand to her forehead as she cowered with guilt. Her loving husband dozed peacefully next to her, completely unaware that his wife was having vivid sex dreams about someone else.

Jesse

"Are you ready?" she asked with a tender smile.

They lay on their overstuffed bed in the middle of the clearing by the creek. The sky was a layer cake of yellow and pink, and the wildflowers swayed gently in the crisp air. He pulled up the blanket and snuggled her as they quietly watched the sun rise through the tall pine trees and over their woods.

"Yep, let's do it," he said. "It's time."

She rolled over and lay her head on his chest. Jesse ran his fingers through Emi's long, soft hair. He leaned down and whispered in her ear.

"I've missed you so much."

He woke with a start, his arms crossed behind his head. Jesse's heart ballooned hopefully as he felt the weight of someone asleep on his chest, but it deflated quickly when he saw that the hair cascading his torso was blond, not brown.

Oh, right. She slept over.

Suddenly, Jesse felt itchy. He smoothly moved out from under her, reaching for his phone on the side table. His screen saver, a picture of his nephew holding his dog, read 3:16 a.m.

He had been waking up at the exact same time every night since he got home from his trip to Pittsburgh. Knowing it was no use trying to put himself back to sleep, Jesse scrolled through post after post of his friends back East. They all seemed to be smiling directly at him, boasting their pretty wives and cute kids. Picture after picture of families on spring break in the Caribbean, a fifth birthday party, a tenth wedding anniversary. He used to look at those posts and feel relieved, unencumbered, free even, without a family of his own. But lately, they left him feeling hollow.

A notification waited for him, and he pressed on the tiny heart icon. His breath caught in his chest, serotonin flooded his brain, and a tsunami of excitement rushed through his veins.

She sent me a friend request.

He looked over to ensure his friend was really asleep. Jesse touched the tiny circle with Emi's warm, cocoa eyes and a wide, dimpled smile. She beamed back at him like she was there in the flesh. He could almost smell her sweet floral scent wafting over him. Everything about her made him anxious, like wading into dark waters.

Jesse hadn't been able to get Emi out of his head since their run-in. And if he were honest with himself—and as a general rule with her, he wasn't—she'd always been in the back of his mind, lurking in the shadows of self-doubt.

Emi's not the twenty-one-year-old girl I knew so long ago. She's a woman now, all grown up like a real adult with a husband and kids. She probably thinks I'm some perpetual man-child clinging on to my youth like all the other desperate, aging bachelors.

He had decided after their run-in that he wouldn't reach out to her. It didn't seem appropriate, even as an old friend. And maybe more so, though he longed to, he just couldn't put himself out there to be hurt by her again.

Because that was exactly what would happen. Emi Klein only ever brought him disappointment, embarrassment, and confusion.

Even still, he couldn't help but look her up the minute he got his nephew in the car. She had changed her name to Emelie Klein Felice, and though he couldn't see pictures of her husband because her profile was private, he didn't want to see them, anyway.

He was bound to be handsome, manly, successful, and doting. Her husband was sure to be perfect. Because she was perfect.

Jesse rolled his eyes at himself, swiped the app away, put his phone down, and turned over to face his late-night friend with benefits. She was beautiful, but she was also young, and they just hadn't hit it off. But after a couple of awkward dates that led nowhere, he was surprised when she'd asked if she could keep his number for what she dubbed 'IMAX and climax.' And as long as that was clear between them, he was happy to oblige. Or at least, he had been. But upon returning to Aspen, something in him had changed.

Why do I keep wasting my time with the wrong women?

He lay on his back and closed his eyes, willing his head to clear for sleep to crawl back in. But he kept circling back to Emi.

Why would she look me up, anyway? Is she just being nice? Does she want to be friends, or is it something more?

But that didn't make sense. True, decades had flown by, but the Emi he met in college didn't seem like the type to cheat. She had always seemed genuine and loyal, which was part of why he had liked her so much.

His curiosity consumed him, and Jesse huffed in defeat.

Fine.

He grabbed his phone, found her request again, and hovered his index finger over 'accept' for a beat before pressing it.

Jesse squinted at her bio. It was empty—except for her birthday. 3/16.

He glanced at the clock again. *Weird.*

And, just like that, his fingers started typing out a message as if driven by their own desire:

Hey, what's up?

He hit send before he could stop himself. Hadn't his sister just lectured him about how he never took chances?

Even though that's probably not what you meant, here you go, Jenna.

Jesse knew none of this would stop his dreams about Emi. The disappointment of reality crashing upon him every morning when he woke was the worst part of them. If anything, messaging her on social media would probably make it worse.

But what does it matter? Dreams don't mean anything anyway. They're just dreams.

Emi

Emi opened her eyes to the smell of bacon frying. She smiled and, with a dramatic groan, stretched like a cat and twisted in her covers. She rolled over, looking for Josh, but found the other side of the bed filled with pillows instead of her husband.

Her phone buzzed on the side table, and Emi fumbled for it, rubbing the sleep out of her eyes. She tapped on the alert to preview her message. It was a photo from Lauren at a peewee soccer game, holding a large thermos of coffee and pretending to cry into the camera.

Death by body shots. I smell like tequila. Hope you're doing better than me, old lady! xo

As the text disappeared, another alert materialized, and Emi froze in terror as her eyes scrolled the words.

Jesse Amato accepted your friend request. Jesse Amato has requested to follow you.

The night before came rushing back. She was going to murder Fae.

Hey, he wrote. *What's up?*

Shit, what would she say? He knew she was married, right? Wait, had she even mentioned that the other day?

Oh God, what if he could tell I was swooning over him, and now he thinks I'm interested?

Emi's head spun like a top. She hadn't fretted this much over a boy since college. Even in the early days with Josh, she hadn't stressed about what he thought. In fact, Jesse was the only boy who had ever made her sweat like this.

"Breakfast is ready, sleepyhead." Josh's voice rang out from the staircase and cut through her thoughts like glass. She jolted up and stuffed her phone under her pillow with the dread of a teenage boy about to be caught with porn.

Wait, why am I freaking out?

It was all perfectly normal. An innocent run-in, followed by a polite social media exchange. Josh knew she had guy friends, and she had never given him any reason to question her. Everything was fine. Totally, ordinarily, boringly, fine.

But Emi still hid her phone under the pillow as she tried to ignore the sinking feeling in her stomach she only got when she was lying to herself.

Dragging herself out of bed, she threw her hair into a haphazard topknot, then walked down the polished dark wood stairs in fuzzy socks and a pair of Josh's plaid boxers. She felt a bit better, but her body's energy tank was depleted from the festivities of the night before. Breakfast was beckoning her, like the promise of a gas station to her sputtering car.

Emi smiled as she passed the sectional in the living room, where Liam lay happily under a blanket, watching cartoons, little legs resting lazily over the dog. She turned into the kitchen to find Josh and Stevie Wonder belting out some of his old hits over the protests of a mortified Violet. Josh was enjoying himself tremendously, holding the spatula as a microphone while intermittently flipping pancakes.

His face lit up as Emi entered. Without missing a beat, he ditched the mic and sang over to the espresso machine, where he picked up the latte that was waiting for her. Letting the pancakes brown a little too long, he grinned as he grabbed her by the hand and spun her around the kitchen.

Maddie jumped from the couch and ran to the back door, barking excitedly. Two seconds later, Jack bounded in with a pink nose on a mission, mud flying up behind him.

"I'm just getting my glove," he declared as he ran through the kitchen and flung open the garage door. He disappeared only for a moment before emerging with an old baseball mitt. Mission completed, he made sure to grab a handful of bacon off the counter and then jogged back out into the sunshine.

"I am so lucky," Josh whispered. Emi opened her mouth to respond, but the words got stuck in her throat, so she forced a smile until she could get them out.

"Me, too," she finally managed. As she looked into his endearing eyes, she knew how blessed she was.

So, why is it suddenly so hard to say it back?

"Keep up," Emi called.

Dew was practically dripping off the little green buds that sprouted from the tall trees, lining her favorite walking trail. The birds had just begun their northward migration and were chirping loudly, each with a different spring song.

"No, you slow down!" Fae shouted as she jogged to catch up.

"It's not me. It's the dog," Emi laughed. Maddie's tongue flopped out of her mouth as she strangled herself, trying to pull faster, panting with excitement. "Did you have fun last night?"

"I did," Fae said. "It was so nice to do something with girlfriends for a change. I never felt like I could go out when I was with Tyler. Anytime I tried, he would always ruin it somehow."

"He was so weirdly jealous of anyone in your life. Do you remember how he would always send you texts threatening to leave you whenever we were together? What a fucking drama queen." Emi pursed her lips and slowed her stride, letting Maddie know to take it easy.

"He was definitely the most insecure about you. He had been saying little things here and there, trying to plant seeds and get you out for years."

"Why, though?"

"Because he knew having you in my life made me stronger, and he needed me weak. We have a healthy relationship, and he was trying to control me while you just wanted me to be happy and advocate for myself."

She sighed. "The worst part about my marriage, though, was the kids. On some level, I always knew he was a narcissist, and I wasn't comfortable leaving him with the girls for too long. He would say the worst things to them sometimes."

Emi looked at her. "That was the worst part?"

"He wasn't physically abusive to them, even if he just hadn't gotten there yet. But I felt like it was just a matter of time until they started standing up to him, and then who knows what would have happened." Fae shook her head in disbelief. "I can't believe how much of my life I wasted trying to manage that man's ego."

"It's okay, Fae. We're not even halfway through our lives. You have so much more time. It wasn't all for nothing," Emi said. "I know I say this all the time, but I'm so glad you left, for everyone's sake."

The path led to a wooden bridge crossing a small lake. They sat on a bench overlooking the water, drinking their take-out coffees, and quietly absorbed the peacefulness of nature around them. Emi watched a couple of turtles stir just under the glass surface, and a family of ducks floated by as Maddie lay down at their feet. A few joggers came and went, then a family with kids on scooters.

Fae broke the silence. "So, are you going to answer him back, or what?"

"Jesse? No. I don't think so."

"You are such a liar. We both know that I know you better than that."

As Emi frowned, a man in gray sweatpants jogged toward them, out for a late morning run. None of them paid each other much mind. But the moment he passed her, just for a split second, Emi caught a glimpse of his profile, and a lightning strike of recognition zapped her brain. She twisted around on the bench and watched as he kept going, unblinking.

No fucking way.

The jogger rounded the little bridge to the other side of the lake where she could get a better look at him. Emi unclenched her body and breathed a sigh of relief as his features seemed to morph, and she could see it wasn't Jesse.

Fae laughed at her strained expression. "Take a picture, it'll last longer."

"What? Shut up, Fae," she sputtered, "I thought I knew him."

That is the second time in just a few days I could have sworn I saw Jesse completely out of nowhere.

A pair of birds cut her anxiety short as they flitted happily through the trees, playing a game of tag. She watched as each one took turns, letting the other almost catch them, their blue feathers outstretched.

Suddenly, it all added up. Like a detective in the last moments of a mystery, all the obvious puzzle pieces that had been easily passed over began to fall into place.

Her dream from the night before came rushing back, with visions of Jesse's hands running over her body. But it hadn't been just some regular old Freudian sex dream. It was immersive, all-encompassing, worlds-colliding, passionate love. Emi could feel the emotions and electric connection wash over her like a tidal wave, as intensely as if it had been real. She closed her eyes and could still sense his weight on top of her and his wanting breath on her skin.

And another dream slipped in, from a few nights before, on her birthday. She could see Jesse's whole face now, not just his dark eyes, smiling at her from under tall pines. Yes, that was him, too. She was sure of it.

As if someone had run a knife through the strange canvas she found herself pondering over, her epiphany was dashed by the thought of her sweet, unsuspecting husband waiting for her at home.

Emi looked over at Fae, who was absentmindedly petting the dog. She wanted to confide in her best friend all the odd coincidences and steamy dreams, just like she normally would. She opened her mouth but couldn't find a starting point. There wasn't anything to tell because nothing had actually happened, except maybe that she was in the early stages of losing her mind.

Okay, what the hell is going on with me?

CHAPTER THREE

2003

It was Thirsty Thursday at the University of Pittsburgh, and Emi was hiding behind a group of people standing by the bar.

Fae and their crew of girlfriends had just bopped off to request songs and flirt with the DJ, but Emi declined their offer to tag along. There wasn't much worse, in her opinion, than the inflated ego of a college disc jockey. But once alone, she found herself in a pickle.

Cowering with her tiny plastic cup, trying to fade into a dark corner until reinforcements returned, Emi peered suspiciously around the room. She could have kicked herself for not going with her friends when she spotted Max. His eyes darted from one girl to the next, and she knew he was looking for her. Aggravation at his persistence and nervousness of public confrontation had Emi on the run.

Is this kid ever going to take a hint?

After she broke things off with him, Max had popped up outside of her sociology class, in the library during her Italian study group, and walking down the street outside her apartment. He would deny any and all accusations, of course, but Emi's bullshit detector couldn't be fooled. Coincidence it was not.

Emi had managed to dodge him at every turn. She stayed back and talked to her sociology professor after class until he left. She hid behind a bookshelf, begging her study buddies with a silent finger to her lips not to give her away. And Fae had stuffed her back through their apartment door when they were stopped short on their way to the grocery store.

And now he was in her favorite bar, on her favorite night, exactly where he knew she would be.

Emi panicked as she realized she had lost sight of him in the crowd. He could be anywhere. He could be right behind her.

A tap landed on her shoulder, and she jumped a foot in the air.

"Holy fucking shit!" Emi whipped around, eyes wide, sure the jig was up. Except she tripped on the landing, lurching forward into a pair of strong arms, and her rum and Diet Coke cascaded all over a hard, broad chest.

Shoved up against it, Emi had nowhere else to look but right at her mess. What was once a crisp white T-shirt, doused with cola stains and the neon glow of black lights, was now a Jackson Pollock.

Her eyes swept upward, excruciatingly slow, to find a face that went with the body, and she sank like quicksand into a pair of warm, black eyes.

"Shit, I didn't mean to frighten you. I just wanted to know what time it is. I'm really sorry," he blurted.

But Emi couldn't answer. Her brain was buffering. Somewhere, deep in her mind, the scent of pine was stirring up memories of long afternoons spent playing in the shade of the evergreen trees behind her parents' lake house. As a broad smile crept across the stranger's mouth, Emi felt dizzy.

Any thoughts of Max were long gone. They stared at each other momentarily, then burst into laughter as if sharing the same mind.

"I'm really sorry. I didn't mean to. Oh shit, you're covered," Emi said sheepishly.

"Nah, it's okay. I scared you. Besides, I look good in," he tugged at his T-shirt and smelled it, "rum."

Emi tried blotting him with cocktail napkins, but the attempt was futile. He gently took her hand and held it still on his chest to let her know she could stop fussing.

She felt the beat of his heart, and in some strange, biological twist, it seemed to sync with hers, the two of them thumping into one. His thick, warm hand lit her skin on fire. Emi had never been speechless in her life, but here she was without a witty word to say.

"I really was just going to ask for the time. My phone died," he said as he held up the black screen. Blushing, she reached for hers, illuminating the inside of her purse with neon green.

"It's twelve-oh-seven," she answered.

"That's my lucky number," he said.

"What? Twelve-oh-seven is your lucky number?" Emi snickered. "Okay, sure."

"I mean seven is my lucky number. It's my birthday. Seven-seven."

Emi's disbelieving look didn't budge.

"Really!" His boyish laugh was gleeful and deep, like church bells in her ears. "July seventh. It's my birthday, I swear."

She cocked an eyebrow. "So, you're a Cancer?"

"Is that a bad thing?"

"Not necessarily," she said coyly.

"And you are?"

"Pisces."

"Ah, then we're soulmates, you and I," he said. Emi was surprised, but she didn't object.

"You know your astrology?"

"I have a little sister. She likes the horoscopes from the back of her magazines. Here, let me buy you another drink. It's the least I can do," he said, reaching up to beckon the bartender.

"Who are you, by the way?"

"I'm Jesse. Who are you?"

"Emi. Emilie."

Jesus, I almost forgot my name.

His smirk was infectious. "It's nice to meet you, Emi Emelie."

"Haha, good one. But I've never seen you before. And, like, I know everybody here."

"Oh, do you?" He chuckled. "Well, this isn't my regular spot. I usually have an early econ class on Fridays, but it was canceled tomorrow. So, my friend asked me to come by and watch his set."

"Oh," Emi said, and she let her guard drop. "Fae—my best friend—just went to say hi to him, I think."

They looked at the DJ booth and watched Fae, wearing the earphones, smiling in all her glory. They locked eyes and she shot Emi a thumbs-up.

Emi and Jesse shared a laugh at their friends' expense and turned back to each other. It could have been the heavy pours, but when their eyes locked again, it was as if all time and space ceased to exist, and everyone and everything around them faded away. And it was just the two of them in that dark bar.

"I'm gonna run to the bathroom to, you know, wash the Captain Morgan off my neck," Jesse said with a starry-eyed smile. "Promise me you'll stay right here. Don't go anywhere."

"Girl Scout's promise," Emi said, pledging a peace sign with her fingers.

He shook his head. "Nope, I'm going to need more than that."

"Alright, fine. Pinky swear," Emi said. He reached out, hooked her delicate hand with his, and brought it close for a kiss. She tingled as every nerve ending screamed with his breath on her skin and he graced her baby finger with soft lips. And with that, Jesse slipped away into the crowd.

Holy shit, what just happened?

Emi couldn't wipe the grin off her face if she tried. Never, ever in her history with boys had she ever been smitten like this.

A quick glance at her phone revealed three missed calls from Max. The clock said it had been an hour, though it felt like she had only been talking to Jesse for a couple of minutes.

Her trance was broken when Fae, wild-eyed and red-faced, snatched Emi by the arm. "We are leaving!" she hissed. "Now!"

"What happened?" Emi asked as she was dragged away. "Wait a sec!"

But Fae had her halfway through the crowd and to the door.

"Please, wait," Emi begged. "Fae, what happened?" She looked desperately over her shoulder at the men's bathroom and then back to the bar, but she didn't see Jesse anywhere.

"He is a fucking creep. Fuck him," Fae muttered.

"Who?"

"Goddamned DJs. They're all the same!"

Her last class let out, and the promise of a weekend had finally set Emi free.

Warm air thawed her winter soul as she made her way through the campus streets and back to her apartment. She passed small groups of students in front of the pizza place, the frat house, and the corner deli, all buzzing over their weekend plans. But as she turned down her street, something pinged in her brain.

Like an elephant sensing a tsunami hundreds of miles out in the open ocean, her body warned her something was about to happen. Goosebumps prickled her arms, and she knew intrinsically whom she had just passed, even before his baritone reached her.

"Emi?"

The sound was deep and sweet, like a foghorn calling her home. She stopped midstep and turned slowly, knowing she would be greeted by his smiling eyes. Dazzled by the sunlight shining through tree leaves, it took a second for his features to sharpen.

It's him!

Before she knew it, she was pulled in for a hug and melted into the warm, familiar scent woven into his sweatshirt. She closed her eyes and forgot herself in the crisp smell of newly cut Christmas trees.

"What's up?" Jesse asked.

In the blink of an eye, déjà vu coursed through her limbs and tingled into her brain. Something about this moment felt so familiar but also far away, like a dream in a past life.

Was it the cast of the midday light or the fresh spring breeze he rode in on? She wasn't sure, but it was definitely him, with those dark eyes that shook her, and the shape of his lips curled into a boyish smirk. Yes, she had done this all before, somewhere.

"Hey," Emi managed to get out. "Wait, do you live here?"

"Nah, I'm just leaving a friend's place," Jesse said.

"Fae and I live at the end of the street. What a coincidence."

"You know, I've been told there are no such things as coincidences."

They beamed into each other's dumbstruck stares. The exchange was so intimate that, for a moment, a vision flashed before her eyes of them lying in bed, warm and content under the covers with large, snow-capped mountains glistening through the window behind.

Jesse broke first. "Can I walk you home?"

He reached for her backpack and swung it over his shoulder. Emi couldn't help but blush at the sight of such a big guy carrying her books for her, and she allowed her guard to drop just to indulge in his sweet nature. At that moment, it struck her that she hadn't felt comfortable enough to be vulnerable with someone for a long time.

Most college boys were pompous and posturing, constantly overcompensating for their complete and utter fear of rejection. They looked upon her beauty and intelligence with clouded intentions of possession and ownership, wanting something from her. They were looking to cash in, whether it was sex, attention, or status. Every boy she had known since high school was so obviously self-serving and green behind the eyes. But, unfortunately for her, Emi was straight as they came, and thus, boys were a necessity.

But with Jesse, even in their limited interactions, it was like they'd been together since the inception of time. Emi was safe with him. She was seen. And the way he gazed at her was so reverent, so genuinely adoring, she felt like she was the most beautiful thing he had ever seen. As if he wasn't looking to exploit but to nurture.

For God's sake, am I really this smitten over a guy I just met?

They bantered easily to the end of the street, stopping in front of a small, rickety blue house. A pink cherry tree was budding outside, and two plastic chairs sat on the small porch.

"Well, this is it," she said. "Thanks for walking with me." But she didn't want him to go, and he didn't move to leave.

"Anytime. I'm glad I ran into you."

As if on cue, they both opened their mouths and began to talk at the same time. He allowed her to speak first.

"Sorry! I was going to say, I'm done for the day. Do you want to hang out for a little? I can drop my stuff off."

Jesse's face lit up. "Sure."

"Okay. Well, in that case, come in. I'm just going to drop my backpack and maybe grab a sweatshirt. We could go to the conservatory if you have your student ID."

"Phipps? I've never been there," Jesse said.

"Oh, well, we have to fix that."

The old Victorian house had been neglected over the years by countless college students, and it shifted and creaked as they made their way through the hallway. Jesse followed Emi to the first doorway on the right, where she came to a sudden stop.

Streams of fairy lights cascaded over the once grand walls of a small room. Above the couch, a plastic lei had been taped around a Tupac poster, along with scattered photos of Fae, Emi, and their many friends. Smiles beamed back at her from beach weeks, house parties, prom, and even a few from when they were little girls.

Someone was on the couch, cocooned in a large comforter, snoring lightly through *Days of Our Lives*. Suddenly, Fae's voice broke the silence from under the lump of blanket.

"Em, you missed it. Bo's in trouble for fucking up the stakeout. He's gone full rogue. And Roman is . . . ahh!"

She sat up quickly, startled to see a man in her hallway.

"Oh my God!" she shrieked, pulling the comforter off her head and flattening her wild blond hair.

Emi twisted around to shoot Jesse a knowing grin. "You remember Fae."

"So, Fae seems cool," Jesse mused after shutting Emi's front door behind him.

"Yeah. She's like my second sister. We've been best friends since we were little," Emi said, setting course for the conservatory.

"Wow, really?"

"Yeah. When her dad died, though, she became more like family. She ate dinner with us most nights, slept over all the time. We went to sleep-away camp together for years. Basically, Fae was with us every moment she could be."

"That's really nice. And you two even made it to college together."

"Well, we didn't have to go far. We grew up like ten minutes away, in Squirrel Hill. What about you? Where are you from?"

"Upstate New York, Rochester. I also have a younger sister. She's actually set to come to Pitt in the fall after she graduates high school."

"That's so sweet," Emi said. "So you can look out for her?"

"That was the plan, but I was just accepted to Cornell for grad school."

Emi's heart dropped a little. "Oh, you're graduating this year?"

"Yep, and a scholarship to Ivy League would be really dope for my career. It would be pretty dumb to turn it down."

"What are you going for?"

"Finance. We grew up watching my mom struggle with us and two jobs. So, I'm going to have enough money to take care of her one day, and my sister, too."

Emi almost stumbled over her own feet, her head spinning with a vision triggered by his last words. She saw herself holding Jesse's hand, bursting with joy and pride, as he passed his mom the keys to the lovely shaker house they just bought for her. Tears in his mother's eyes brought tears to her own, and the three of them embraced right there in the front yard.

"I have to let Cornell know soon, but I'm torn. I feel like it would be good for Jenna if I was here. Our dad left early on and I've kind of raised her in a way, you know? I could give her some stability and keep all the creeps away."

"Oh, I'm sorry to hear that. You must've been through a lot together."

"It's whatever." He shrugged. "But like, I know she needs me. So, I'm still not sure if I should just stay at Pitt or what."

"Yeah, that's a tough one. But on the other hand . . ." Emi smiled and cocked an eyebrow. "You're saying there's hope for me yet?"

"Yeah," Jesse laughed. "There's hope."

They took turns blushing down shady streets lined with thin row houses that had long before been chopped up into shabby tenements for poor college kids. Rap and pop music thumped through rickety windows that had been thrown open and propped up to welcome in the warmth of the new season.

Emi and Jesse shared stories of childhood friends, family, and home, marveling at how they could finish each other's sentences. They were both shocked to find they had so much in common. They frequented the same restaurants and bars on campus and even had mutual acquaintances.

Emi's nerve endings scorched red-hot, painfully aware of how closely his body came to brushing up against her.

Please reach out and hold my hand!

They teased each other around a large stone fountain where couples sat with their feet in the water, then cut through a sprawling courtyard littered with students lying in the newly green grass, soaking in the sun, or chatting on benches. The delicious aroma wafting from the line of food trucks in front of the Carnegie Library made Emi's stomach rumble, but she was too excited to even think about eating.

After twenty of the longest minutes Emi could remember, they came upon a concrete bridge adorned with a safety fence on one side. The chain-link shimmered in the sunlight with hundreds of silver bicycle locks, the metal swarming like bees.

"I've always wondered what the deal is with these," Jesse said, nodding to the locks.

"Oh," Emi said, surprised he didn't know. "It's a love lock bridge."

"It's a what?"

"Well, in Paris, there is a bridge called the Pont des Arts. It's a walking bridge over the Seine River that people from all over the world hang locks on, as a symbol of their love for each other. Every square inch is covered with them."

He raised his eyebrows, impressed by her knowledge. "Is this where you tell me you're an architecture major?"

She giggled. "No, I'm actually going for journalism. But it's that I was there a few years ago. There are so many locks on the Pont des Arts that you can't even see the bridge. So, I guess someone from Pittsburgh decided to bite their style and bring it back."

Jesse remained silent, contemplative. She smiled at a bluebird who sang out from its perch on the fence top above.

Jesse

Lush, bright green burst out at them from all corners as Emi and Jesse stepped into the first room of the Phipps Conservatory. He breathed in the jungle air, sweet and thick like molasses. Hundred-year-old palm trees brushed the ceiling of the two-story glass vault above, and tropical flowers sprouted red and orange from big, round leaves down below. A pair of birds who accidentally found their way in called to each other from up high. And two stone paths, one to their left and one to their right, meandered in and out of sight behind large, dewy, prehistoric plants.

He allowed Emi to lead the way, giving him little tidbits of knowledge about the exhibits as they went. He liked it when she explained things to him and could listen to her sweet voice all day. Hearing her chatter on felt so familiar, so right. Like they had already spent a lifetime together. He smiled to himself as he realized he'd never felt so at ease with anyone.

In the Parisian Room, meticulously sculpted hedges pruned in a fleur-de-lis led them down a cobblestone path. Ivy climbed up latticed walls, and Jesse stifled his childish urge to stare when they walked past stone statues of naked women.

Stepping into the Orchid Room was like stepping into the steamy tropics. She took them around a large indoor pond surrounded by every color and kind of orchid known to man. Jesse couldn't tell if it was the humidity beating down on the glass or if it was because Emi grazed him as they walked, but his sweatshirt was damp with sweat, and he tugged at the clinging fabric.

He breathed a sigh of relief in the Desert Room; though it was still hot, the air was thinner and dry. Littered with cacti from one inch to ten feet tall, it contained every size and shape imaginable. There were dark green cacti with yellow spikes, yellow-green cacti with brown spears, white-flowered cacti, and even one that looked like a ten-foot-tall giant squid with razor-sharp tentacles reaching out in every direction.

They strode through the Japanese garden in the outside courtyard, which hosted a koi pond and traditional red maples. Emi stopped on the arched bridge to watch golden fish swim under the glassy water, and the tree's red glow lit her face so brightly that Jesse walked right into one of the posts.

Good one.

Everything about Emi was addictive. Jesse noticed he was beginning to chase her smiles. Needing a continuous fix, he found he was saying anything to keep her giggling, even before the last dimpled grin she wore fell. His stomach fluttered as she laughed easily through the Bonsai Room.

But his delight in Emi's company made way for the sinking weight of inadequacy to settle in as he began to compare himself to her amazing life. She talked about living in Japan for a year as a kid and described the street markets with live eels to pick out for dinner, sushi for breakfast, and what public school had been like—and did so with the same humble, unpretentious tone she used to reminisce about growing up in Pittsburgh and summers on Chautauqua Lake.

Finally, a place I know.

"No way," he blurted. "I love Chautauqua Lake."

"Seriously?"

"Yeah. It's just a couple of hours from Rochester. My family used to vacation there in the summers, too."

"How have we never met before?" she wondered.

"I don't know. It sounds like we've been circling each other in some way for years."

The truth was that his mom barely had enough money to get them to Chautauqua Lake once a year, and only for a long weekend if they were lucky. Jesse was captivated by everything Emi had to say, but his throat went dry when all he could contribute to the conversation was a *wow* or *that's so cool.*

Emi was rich, smart, funny, well-traveled, and maybe the most beautiful girl he had ever seen. There was no way he could keep up with her.

"You know what I mean?" Emi finished her sentence and turned around, looking at him expectantly with those large almond eyes.

"Uh, yeah," he answered, not knowing what he was agreeing to. But he just couldn't concentrate for very long when she was around.

Clearly, she's out of my league. I know it, and I'm sure she does, too.

"This is my favorite room." Emi squealed and clasped her hands, then disappeared through an open doorway. He followed but wasn't sure what she was so excited about. Every other room was like crash-landing on a different planet, but with no exotic plants or pools of water, it was the least interesting of them all.

She turned and waited for him in the underpass of a stone bridge, and his heart almost leaped out of his chest as she slipped her hand in his. It was small and delicate, and her skin was soft and familiar. It fit just right, like the last puzzle piece, as if it were made especially for him to hold.

Jesse thought about kissing her there, in the dark. But she pulled him to the other side, and he realized what that intoxicating smile had been all about.

As they stepped out of the shadows, his mouth dropped, and his gaze shifted from Emi to the elegant wings of every color that fluttered and flapped around her.

Twenty butterflies circled from above and then floated majestically down, gracefully cutting through the air between them. Nothing in his life had been as precious as the look on her face, awestruck and lit up like a little girl's, as she watched one land on his shoulder.

Pure joy emanated from them, and surrounded by such magic, he would have sworn they were the only two people left on earth. A twinge of something in the back of his mind told him to indulge in this moment because he knew he would carry it with him for the rest of his life.

Emi

"Can I buy you an ice cream?" Jesse asked hopefully as they stepped back onto the lock bridge together, heading home.

Emi was relieved and a little giddy that he, too, wasn't ready to say goodbye. "Sure," she said, playing down her eagerness. "Dave and Andy's?"

"Is there any other kind?"

He grinned and led the way, but something seemed to catch Jesse's eye before they reached the other side. He stopped short to look at one of the bicycle locks linked to the fence.

"Look, this one has our initials." He picked up the lock and tilted it toward her. Roughly engraved on the silver was J+E.

Emi took a deep breath as she looked for herself. She stood there for a moment, marveling at its fortuity. But something about the way the light glinted off the metal and how the lock looked clasped in his hand felt familiar, like watching a movie she'd seen a hundred times.

"You said the original bridge is in Paris?" Jesse asked as he turned back to her. Emi nodded.

"Yes. Above the Seine River."

"Well, maybe one day you'll show me in person."

Emi blushed and felt a nervous energy rush through her. She couldn't remember the last time she felt that kind of excitement, if ever.

"Oh yeah?"

"Let me see your wrist."

Emi held up her hand to reveal the black hair band she had been wearing. Jesse gently pulled it off and knotted it tightly around one of the links in the fence.

"That'll have to do. For now."

Shocked by his brazenness, Emi stood there and blinked, not knowing what to say. She felt him coming closer and closer, sure he was going to kiss her.

Finally!

Emi leaned into him, heart thumping. Their lips were a few inches apart, and everything else in the world slipped away.

Until Jesse's phone cut in loudly from his pocket.

They jumped back as their glass bubble shattered around them. Emi gave an awkward laugh, and with the moment spoiled, she motioned that it was okay for him to answer.

"Hello? Yeah. What time? Um," Jesse said as he turned away, trying to shield her from his conversation. Emi pretended she was inspecting the locks and tried to stuff her disappointment down. "You don't have anyone else? What about the new guy? Okay. I guess. Yeah, see you then."

He turned back to her, true agony in his eyes.

"I'm really sorry. That's work. Someone no-showed, and they need me to fill in."

"Oh, no problem. You should totally go. I can walk home myself."

Oh my God, don't listen to me! Please stay!

He inspected her face like he was trying to read between the lines.

"It's fine, really," Emi assured him with a fading smile.

Jesse brought her into his big arms one last time. She didn't want him to let her go.

"Are you sure?" he asked.

"Sure."

No, I am absolutely not.

"We will run into each other again," Emi said with a wink.

"Well, the store I work at closes at nine. Do you want to run into me again tonight, maybe at Murphy's around eleven?"

Emi smiled widely, her dimples as deep as her joy. She muffled her excitement, tucked her hair behind her ear, and answered as casually as she could manage.

"That sounds like that could happen."

The dim Irish pub was packed on that Friday night, even more so than usual since the weather had finally broken. Emi scanned the darkened room the instant she entered, and her stomach flipped with excitement as she locked eyes with Jesse in the back. Snatching Fae's hand, she led their descent through the crowd of rowdy twenty-year-olds, weaving through dollar drafts and shots of Goldschläger. Emi watched his smile creep wider with each step.

"Someone likes you," Fae giggled as she nudged Emi in the ribs.

Jesse met them somewhere in the middle, gave hugs, and introduced his roommate, Matt. They mingled, took a few shots, and played a game of pool. An hour passed like a blink.

"I have to pee," Fae announced, plopping her drink down on the high-top table next to them. "Jesse, can you watch our drinks, please?"

She grabbed Emi's hand before he could respond and yanked her away. They pushed through the swinging door and into the safety of the restroom, and Fae whipped around with a serious look.

"So, you like this kid, yeah?"

"Um. I guess so." Emi tried to sound detached, but she knew Fae could read her smallest micro-mannerisms, even the pitch of her voice. "Why? Do you not like him?"

"No, it's not that. Jesse's cool. But his roommate, Matt—do you guys know each other or something?"

"No, I don't know him. Why?"

Fae hummed to herself in thought and found an empty stall while Emi nervously looked herself over in the mirror.

"Well, every time you talk, he glares at you. He looks real salty, like he's hating on you hard. Are you sure you didn't have a class with him or meet him at a party? Did you hook up with him, maybe?"

"No, I don't think so. That's so weird." Emi craned forward to touch up her mascara. "But Jesse did tell me earlier that they had mutual friends with Max."

"Well, that's a red flag, for sure. Or maybe Matt was that guy who tried to make out with you last year at homecoming?"

"Oh, the guy I shoved into the beer pong table?" The girls laughed. "No. He couldn't be. Could he?"

Fae stepped out of the stall and crept to the door, beckoning Emi closer. Peeking back into the crowd, they watched the boys linger at the bar. Emi's heart melted a little as Jesse steadfastly guarded their drinks.

"Maybe he was the guy you headbutted last year for calling us cunts?" Emi asked.

"Oh my God! Because we won the beer pong tournament?"

"Yes. That was hands down the best moment of my life, by the way," Emi chortled.

"Same! But no, that guy was taller."

Another girl suddenly pulled open the door on them, and they were caught red-handed in their recon mission, almost toppling over onto each other.

"Sorry!" they snickered, pushing back out into the mass of bodies.

Emi immediately began making her way to Jesse, who was waiting for her with a smile. But Fae stopped her.

"Listen. I'm not sure what that's about, but I would watch it with Matt. There's something off there."

"He's probably just jealous or something." Emi shrugged. "You know what petulant little bitches boys are when they aren't the ones getting the attention."

"Last call!" the bartender bellowed as he wiped his sweaty brow and flung a rag over his shoulder, signaling he was ready to be done with the night. Fae swiveled around, wearing her telltale mischievous grin, and clapped her hands on Emi's shoulders.

"Tell Jesse I left you," she whispered in Emi's ear.

"What? Why?"

"Just do it. I know you drove us here, but tell him I left with your keys or something. It'll work. I'll make sure he sees me leaving."

"Fae, make what work?" But before she could elaborate, Matt and Jesse cut through the mob with four Snakebite shots in plastic cups and handed two of them over.

"Got 'em just in time," Jesse said proudly. Fae didn't wait for cheers, throwing hers back quickly.

"Thanks! Peace out, boys. It's been real." And before anyone could protest, she squeezed Emi and trotted out the door.

"What was that about?" Jesse laughed.

"Nothing," Emi sighed with an impressed smile. "That's just Fae being Fae."

The lights above them flickered on and off. Like bugs suddenly exposed from beneath a rock, the crowd recoiled in disapproval. Some drunken idiots booed from the back room. Nonetheless, it was time to leave.

Emi's heart soared as Jesse touched the small of her back and guided her outside. Matt followed in a strange sulk that neither of them wanted to acknowledge. She didn't care about Jesse's dumb friend and didn't want to give him or his attitude any attention. Emi was warm and fuzzy from the drinks and smitten with the prospect of love, and she wasn't going to let Matt ruin it.

"What now?" Jesse asked, yellow light shining through the pub window and dancing in his eyes.

"I'm not really sure. I think Fae took my keys with her. She left so fast that I totally forgot."

"Well then. Our apartment is just around the corner. You can call someone to get you, or you're welcome to sleep over," he said with a concerned smile. "Matt and I share a room, but you can have my bed. I'll sleep in the living room."

Matt rolled his eyes and let out an audible huff. But Jesse looked at him kindly, and he quieted.

The large glass door of Jesse's apartment building closed quietly behind them. They crossed the red-carpeted foyer and went up two flights of stairs, then made a left down a long hallway with thin wooden doors on either side.

Emi's body tingled from head to toe, but she couldn't tell if it was all those shots or déjà vu. She studied each door they passed, wondering if she had been there before, but couldn't come up with anything. Somehow, though, Emi knew they were headed to the last door at the end of the hallway, where Matt stuck his key in the lock. She wasn't sure, but she thought he gave her a side-eye as he turned the deadbolt.

He swung the door in, revealing a typical college boy's apartment. A small kitchen with dingy cabinets opened into a living room with a sixty-inch plasma TV, PlayStation, a dusty old couch, and a loveseat. Half-smoked joints had been left in an ashtray on the coffee table, and a fully stocked bottom-shelf bar was in the corner. Beside it was a glass bong and a stack of red Solo cups.

Emi considered the sofa, then sized Jesse up head to toe. He was easily over six feet tall, with a build to match, and there was no way he could fit himself on the tiny couch he had promised to sleep on.

"You're way too big to fit on that little thing. I can sleep there. No worries," she said as she put her purse on the kitchen table.

"No, I've done it before. It's totally fine. I would be embarrassed to have you sleep on my couch. I insist." He looked so genuine, she knew she would be safe with Jesse. She could feel it.

"Well, this is silly. Why don't we just share your bed? That way, nobody is put out. We're just sleeping, though," she said with a mock finger wag and a smile. "It'll be a pajama party."

The morning was bright, and the blue sheet draped over the top half of the window lit up, casting the white walls in a purple hue. Emi was warm and cozy under the comforter, completely forgetting where she was.

She opened her eyes and was surprised to see another pair, dark like espresso, looking at her from the other side of the bed. Shocked, her hands instinctively checked her body to see if she was clothed. It wouldn't be the first time she had woken up naked in a stranger's bed after a long night of drinking.

Oh, right. I slept over at Jesse's.

"Hey. You sleep okay?"

"Yeah, I actually forgot where I was for a second there." She inhaled the scent of his sheets; it reminded her of a cozy winter morning. "Thanks for letting me stay the night."

I hope I don't still smell like Jägermeister. And ugh, I wish I could brush my teeth.

"Anytime," Jesse replied. Emi felt blood rush to her cheeks.

"I'll call Fae to come get me," she murmured, recalling their ruse from the night before.

"Sure, no hurry. I don't have to work today, so I'm just hanging out."

"I do have to head home, though. My sister's in town, and she's picking me up later."

"Tell me about your family," Jesse said. Emi was flattered.

Is he trying to get me to stay?

"Well, Fae and I live together, but when they're traveling, I stay at my parents' house a lot. Rose comes home to visit every so often, but she lives in New York."

"Where do your parents go?"

"Everywhere. It's more like, where don't they go? My mom's an anthropology professor at Pitt, and my dad is dean of their political science department. They're always off doing research, going to conferences, teaching, and taking sabbaticals. When I was younger, I would go with them. It was a cool way to grow up. It really shaped my worldview and made me more open-minded."

"I bet. I'm super jealous." The bridge of his nose flushed, and his gaze drifted to the ceiling, as if he didn't like the words he was about to say. "I've barely been able to leave Rochester. One day, I'm going to put my feet on every continent."

"What's first on your list?" Emi asked. Almost immediately, Jesse's attention snapped back to her, his easy passion restored.

"Italy, for sure. I feel like it's always called to me for some reason. Like something's waiting there for me. My mom's family is from Capri, and I promised her when I was little that one day I'd take her and my sister."

"You're going to love it, Jesse. Italy is awesome," she promised him. "I spent last summer there, and it was the most romantic place I've ever been. I think I must have lived there in a past life or something because I have a recurring dream of the Amalfi Coast. I'm sitting in a blue dress next to a cliffside above the ocean," she trailed off, then remembered herself. "The only downside was I gained like five pounds on pasta and wine, though, so watch out."

Jesse reached over and playfully pinched what he could get from the sliver of tummy that lay under her crop top.

"What? There's nothing there." He smirked.

Emi giggled and squirmed away. "If anyone else had done that, I would have smacked them."

"Sorry. Just—I don't get how you could think about that, seriously. You're just, like, the perfect girl," Jesse added. She craved his touch again.

Is this it? Are we finally going to kiss?

But something behind Jesse on the windowsill caught her attention. A bluebird appeared on the other side of the glass, like it had been conjured out of thin air. It looked at her with purpose and cocked its head to one side as if it had something important to say.

Emi didn't realize until it was too late that Jesse's head was coming at her fast, and, still watching the bird, she flinched as his soft lips touched hers. Before she could react, his tongue slid across her front teeth, and she fumbled any attempt at an intimate moment. Jesse immediately recoiled, and a look of confusion crossed his face.

A tidal wave of mortification washed over her. Emi opened her mouth to explain, but when she glanced back to the window, the bird was gone.

Suddenly, a loud, wet snore cut through the tension like a knife, and Matt tossed in his bed on the other side of the room. They were thankful to laugh.

"Uh, I'll be right back," Jesse said. He slid out of bed and out of the room, leaving Emi to cringe alone. The weight of deep regret settled in her chest.

Fuck.

CHAPTER FOUR

2022

Anytime Emi felt confused or frustrated with her life, she would grab her sneakers and go for a run. So, there she was, jogging alongside the Monongahela River. Its yellow bridges led to the stadiums on her right, the large fountain in Point State Park on her left, and the tall buildings of downtown Pittsburgh, picturesquely behind it against the blue sky.

It was a beautiful day in the city. The cherry trees were budding with little pink flowers, and the grass had begun to turn green again. She felt the dullness of winter giving way to the new life of spring and breathed in the fresh air that rejuvenated her spirit. But even so, she couldn't quite shake the dread.

Jesse had become, once again, omnipresent in her life. It was as if he were a thunderstorm lurking in the distance, waiting to ruin her happy family picnic.

Everywhere she went, every interaction seemed to circle back to him. She would catch a glimpse of his smile on some TV actor, overhear his name in a conversation at the grocery store, or suddenly hear a song that reminded her of him. Since her birthday, she had woken up in cold sweats every morning, torn harshly from intimate moments with him in the realm of sleep. She couldn't outrun the thousand unexpected small cuts that left her tortured by tiny knives of coincidence, seemingly hidden around every corner.

Emi wished she could talk to Rose or Fae about it. But it was too weird. Even if she could find the words, she was sure she would sound crazy. And she'd have to admit to them, and maybe even to herself, that she'd allowed Jesse to take over. And that she'd embarrassingly slipped back into some overly dramatic pubescent loop: *What did all of these strange events mean? Was he looking for just friendship, and why do I care?* And lastly, *Should I answer his message or not?*

She rolled her eyes at the melodrama of it all. Yes, at forty, she was sixteen again.

What would I even say?

I'll tell him the truth—duh—that I'm happily married with three beautiful kids. And anyway, he was probably just being polite because I sent him a friend request first.

But no. She needed to leave it. She would say nothing.

Emi slowed to a walk and sat on one of the large concrete pedestrian steps overlooking the water. Her mind was churning out a million questions all at once, jamming her thoughts like paper in a printer.

It was impossible, after all this time, that she could still be carrying a torch for this guy, right?

No way. Josh is the love of my life. Yes, he is. Definitely.

Life had fallen into place when she and Josh started dating. Once she decided to give him a chance, they fell swiftly and deeply in love, passion paired equally with friendship and mutual respect.

From there, everything just seemed to work itself out, like puzzle pieces fitting together one after another. Without much intention or thought on her part, she'd been swept up in fate's current. The business of life and all its babies, school functions, family holidays, and everything in between kept her spinning, and sometimes Emi felt like life was flying past her so quickly she couldn't grab on to any of it.

Maybe none of this was about Jesse. But that idea scared her even more because maybe she was secretly unhappy.

Emi swallowed hard. If ever there was a time to face her fears head-on, it was now.

Am I satisfied? Have I allowed myself to become another boring carpool mom with nothing in my life besides laundry and bake sales?

Emi felt her throat close and forced a deep breath.

Liam was going to kindergarten in the fall, and she could start thinking of herself again. Maybe even start writing more. She missed that side of her. Her marriage wasn't perfect, but they were happy and in love, which was more than a lot of people could say. And the kids were her world. Sure, she was tired and overstimulated and sometimes locked herself in her walk-in closet to cry. But no one ever said motherhood was easy, and they fulfilled her in ways that she never could have imagined. She was happy.

As Emi watched the river ripple, her confusion began to lift, and a slow calm washed over her. Maybe all she needed was to take a little inventory. Emi closed her eyes and inhaled another deep, cleansing breath. But something sticky still lingered in her chest.

Had her insecurities manifested these strange occurrences, or was there something deeper with Jesse—some connection she had yet to discover?

As her eyes opened, she almost jumped off her seat.

A brightly colored bluebird sat beside her on the concrete step, bobbing his head as if to answer.

Emi's heart soared as she watched Liam strut across the wooden platform like a little man, surrounded by twelve other five-year-olds.

"This is a milestone for our class." His teacher beamed as the kids came to a stop in their rehearsed spots. "It's their last art show here at Rosemont Academy, and I, for one, am so honored and touched that you allowed me to be here with them. I've known most of your children since they were two years old, and now here they are, about to head off to kindergarten, and I couldn't be prouder. After the show, please peruse their artwork from this year. Now, without further ado, our pre-K spring recital begins with, 'You Are My Sunshine.'"

Just as the kids began their song, Josh snuck into his seat, loosening his tie and draping his arm around her. Emi stifled her annoyance that he was late—again—to Liam's show.

Whatever, he's here. And that's what matters.

Liam, her last baby, glowed as he sang his little heart out on stage. Her eyes teared up with nostalgia, and her cheeks ached from smiling.

She and Josh had done it: three kids, potty trained and out of preschool. That was no small feat, and she couldn't be prouder of the two of them. They were such a good team.

But Emi's heart thrashed when, as the program finished and the students shuffled back across the stage single file, Liam cried out in pain and buckled to his knees. The next children in line, not paying attention, tumbled over him, one on top of the other, with the coordination of baby giraffes.

The horrified pre-K teacher tried to rein in the commotion, but as there were now six kids crying loudly in front of their parents, she had completely lost control. Emi swooped in and scooped up Liam, finding the culprit of his agony: a bee stinger sticking out of a quarter-sized lump on his leg.

"Oh, poor baby," she tutted. "It's just a bee sting." But Liam only screamed louder.

"It's okay, honey. I know it hurts, but it'll be all right, I promise," she said with the coolness of a seasoned mom. "Josh, I'm going to take him to the bathroom. Be right back."

After five full minutes of Liam's tortured screams echoing from the bathroom and down the hall, Emi finally calmed Liam down. He staggered out in dinosaur bandages, fished from the bottom of her purse, with all the despondency of an injured war vet.

They rejoined the crowd at the art show, blending into happy families who were proudly pointing at the few hundred handmade crafts adorning the walls. Emi was surprised to see that Josh, however, wasn't waiting for them. She thought for sure he'd be there with a big smile on his face, ready to throw Liam on his shoulders and make it all better. But she didn't see him anywhere.

"Hey, have you seen Josh?" Emi asked a mom friend who passed her by. But she shrugged and shook her head.

There were no messages waiting on her phone. So, Emi held Liam's hand and began the tour, sure that Josh was just chatting it up with someone and would find them eventually.

Piece after piece, painting after painting, her calm dissipated into hot fury.

Where the hell could he be?

Finally—with no husband in sight—her phone rang.

"Where are you?" she demanded, voice hushed.

"What do you mean? I'm at home. I thought it was over."

Josh was completely oblivious to her anger. Emi's blood boiled.

"You missed the art show," she whispered. "That was the whole point."

"I saw it all on the way out. Liam did a great job."

"Are you fucking kidding me?"

"I mean, we drove separately. I just thought you'd leave soon, too. Anyway, I was hoping you could pick up my prescript—"

Emi punched the red end-call button. She was so pissed off she had to hang up on him before she cursed him out in front of the whole school.

"Where's Daddy?" Liam asked, looking up at her. She sighed and smiled brightly.

"He's going to meet us at home, honey. But don't worry, he saw all your artwork. Anyway, let's have a cupcake and see your friends, and then we can get going, too."

Emi slammed the garage door behind her. She haughtily dropped a plethora of crap in the middle of the mudroom in protest, refusing to put it away. With each item she had plucked from the car floor; Jack's dirty baseball cleats, various school papers, Liam's half-melted Ring Pop, and Violet's empty Starbucks cup—her anger grew.

Everyone left all their shit in the car again, knowing I would have to pick it all up and put it away. Well, not today. I'm not their fucking maid.

As she stomped toward the stairs, Josh emerged from the office.

"I'm sorry, babe. I didn't think it would be a big deal," he said in his most convincing, helpless husband voice.

"You left your son's last pre-K art show without saying goodbye. How the hell could that not be a big deal?"

"I thought it was over," Josh said, looking bewildered. He always made that face when he stumbled, headfirst, into the great unknown territory of *my wife is mad, but I don't know why*.

She loathed that look.

"Josh, you also saw him get stung by a bee and have a fucking meltdown in front of the entire school. He took out five other kids like dominoes. You watched me take him to the bathroom. I literally said I'd be right back.

But you couldn't wait three minutes for us? I felt like a fucking idiot chasing after my husband and asking everyone if they saw you. And don't you think Liam wanted to show you the art he's been working on all year? That was a big deal for him."

Josh stared blankly.

"Not to mention, I had to lug all forty pounds of Liam and his backpack—sweating profusely in full sun, next to the main road with cars flying past us—back to my car. It was not cool."

"Why didn't you just park in the lot?"

"It was full."

"Oh, well, why didn't you just make him walk?"

Emi thought her head might explode. He looked so innocent and yet was so stupid.

"Oh, yeah, honey. Why didn't I think of that?" she mocked. "Because his fucking leg just got stung by a giant bee!"

"Well, he would have walked for me."

Does this man have a death wish?

"I'm sorry," Josh said calmly. "Next time you need my help, just call me, honey."

"No, dickwad. Next time, just fucking wait for your wife!"

Violet rounded the corner and stood at the top of the stairs. She pursed her lips and rolled her eyes at her phone, engulfed in her own drama. Josh took the opportunity to slip back into the office, no doubt relieved Emi was already dealing with the next item on her endless to-do list.

"Mom, I need you to take me to Leah's," she demanded. Emi shot her a look. "What? She has my white hoodie, and I need it for tonight. Prestley's taking me out for dinner. Oh, yeah, and we need a ride. There and back. Like, now."

"Violet, I cannot give you a ride."

"Why not?"

"Because I'm busy. Next time, ask me more than two minutes in advance."

"Whatever," Vi scoffed. "What's your problem?"

"My problem is there's only one of me, and I can't do everything for everyone all the time."

"Honey?" Josh yelled from the office. "Did you get my prescription?"

"Oh, my God! You're all trying to kill me!" Emi bellowed.

It was like watching an explosion from inside the volcano. She knew how melodramatic it was, how crazy she must've seemed—she sounded like *she* was the angsty teen of the house—but it was too late. Tears were stinging her eyes, and she ran up the stairs, past her disgruntled daughter, and slammed her bedroom door.

"Don't be mean to Dad," Violet barked at her from the hallway. "He didn't do anything to you. Just because you're on your period doesn't mean you can take it out on the rest of us."

Emi threw herself on the bed and cried.

It was impossible to be everyone's everything all the time. Even when she waited on them hand and foot, cleaned the house, did the laundry, cooked healthy meals, carpooled, and comforted them—all with a

Stepford smile—nobody cared. They didn't even notice. They only noticed when she couldn't or wouldn't.

How has my life ended up belonging to everyone else but me?

Emi pulled her phone out of her back pocket and opened her messages. She stared at Jesse's words on the screen for a few minutes and began typing.

"Hey! I'm here!" Rose yelled as the door slammed shut.

"I'm on the porch." Emi's voice echoed to the front of the house. She had been waiting anxiously; she knew it was time to confide in Rose. If there was anyone on the planet she could trust with a secret, it was her sister.

"Where is everyone?" Rose asked, walking through the deserted kitchen and out onto the porch. "It's eerie in here without all the noise and chaos."

"Josh took the kids out to dinner and a movie. It's so nice outside, I thought we could sit back here."

Rose eyed the frosty bottle of white wine waiting for her on the coffee table.

"Oh my God, thank you. Work has been insane," Rose said as Emi handed her a glass. "Let me tell you about the one guy who's cyberstalking his ex. Holy shit, can you please take the geo-tracking off all your phones? And shut off your Alexa while you're at it. That contraption's such a nosy bitch. I guess it was recording soundbites of her conversations, and he figured out how to tap into them. I mean, seriously, how dumb are we, though? We invented robots to spy on us."

The moment Rose looked up at Emi, her rant snuffed itself out. She could tell something was up. "What's wrong?"

"Sit down. I have to tell you something." Rose suddenly looked worried. The patio lights above them clicked on as twilight set in.

"You've been putting money away like I told you, right?"

"What? No, Rosie. Josh and I are fine. He's great. I mean, annoying at times, but we are good."

"Okay, then what's this about?"

"Do you remember I told you about bumping into that guy, Jesse? Well, Fae sent him a friend request from my account. We've messaged a few times."

"What does that mean?" Rose asked skeptically.

Emi hesitated, then pushed her phone to Rose, who picked it up and read the message exchange. Her eyebrow quirked.

"This all looks very nice and normal, Em. I don't see what the problem is."

"I told you; it's me. I'm the problem. He keeps liking all my stuff, and it's driving me crazy."

"Um, isn't that the whole point of social media?"

"Yeah, but it's more than that. I find myself thinking about what I'm posting because he'll see it and wonder if he'll like it. And, like, every time I get a notification from him, I just panic. I'm thirteen years old all over again.

And then I've been having these dreams, and I don't know why. But I'm feeling so guilty about all of it," Emi confessed.

"Hm. Josh knows you ran into Jesse at baseball, right?" Emi nodded as she took a sip of her wine. "Does he know about talking to him over social, or is that a secret?"

"No, I told him. Obviously, he doesn't know my feelings about all of it. But he knows Jesse's an old friend and that we reconnected online."

"Okay. So, then, what kind of dreams are you having? Like, sex dreams?"

Emi fidgeted in her seat.

"Yes," she answered with trepidation. "But not just sex dreams. Other dreams, too. I keep having this recurring dream that we're madly in love, living in a forest or something. But it feels so real."

Emi decided that the moment of silence from her sister was all the validation she needed to absolutely hate herself. But instead of condemning her, Rose burst out in laughter.

"Is that it?" Rose balked when Emi nodded. "That's nothing. I dream about my exes all the time. I dream about that asshole, Sandra. And sometimes I dream that I haven't graduated college. I dreamt once that I beat up Carrie Gardener, that skank who outed me in fifth grade, and I ran her dog over with a car."

Emi croaked out a laugh. Rose put her wine glass down and slid closer.

"I even dreamt once when you were pregnant with Jack that I microwaved him. I microwaved him because I thought he was cold. Like, I dreamt I put your baby in the fucking microwave. None of that means anything, Em."

"Okay, but anytime I've dreamt about exes, I was running away from them. With Jesse, they're so real and passionate. Intimate, even. When I wake up, I half expect him to be in my bed instead of Josh. And, like, honestly, sometimes, before I open my eyes, I try to go back because it feels so, I don't know, good. I mean, Rosie, isn't that fucking crazy? If I'm not a horrible person, what else would it mean?"

"Nothing. It means nothing. Look, you are my best friend and baby sister, and I love you, so I say this with love. You are spiraling. Like, seriously. Let pathos go already."

Emi rolled her eyes. "You're only saying that because you've got big-sister goggles on. You are completely unable to see me as anything but a catastrophizing six-year-old."

"No, seriously, you are so dramatic. You always have been. I mean, what baby has colic for an entire year? At some point, it was like, okay, we get it, enough already. And remember that time you told Mom I almost pushed you out of our bedroom window at the lake house?"

"You did almost push me out of the window. I could have died!"

"There was a screen," Rose rebutted flippantly. "You were so paranoid after that you convinced yourself I was trying to kill you for like a whole month, and you wouldn't come near me. See what I mean? You have always gotten yourself all worked up over nothing."

Rose nudged her with a smile, then cleared her throat.

"More importantly, is the sex good? I mean, I know it's with a man, so it can't be that good," she said. Emi huffed her displeasure.

"Can you please try to take this seriously? Just for two minutes? You're all jokes over here, but I'm about to cry."

"Okay, fine. For two minutes. When did these dreams start?"

"The morning of my birthday, I think. Which was the day I ran into him. So, a few weeks now. Everything just popped off from there. But it's not just dreams, either. Weird coincidences all day, every day, keep reminding me of him, too. Rosie, stop smiling like that. I'm serious."

"I admit it's weird," Rose said, trying to hide her amusement. "But it's classic anxiety. You're having intrusive thoughts again. Remember how bad it got after you had Liam? What was that thing your doctor told you?"

"My anxiety is chronic, but my ass is iconic?"

Rose spat out her drink. "Yes, but no."

"She said that I have an overactive imagination." Emi sighed.

"That's right. You're just reading too much into it, is all. Not everything means something."

"So, you don't think I'm crazy or a horrible person?" Emi asked earnestly.

"No, Em, I don't think you're a horrible person. You're totally normal, I promise. Unfriend him, and you'll probably never think of Jesse Amato ever again. Once you stop freaking out, your brain will fixate on something else to drive you crazy.

Honestly, honey, you have a great family and a great marriage. And you and Josh are the happiest damn couple I know. You're like newlyweds still. You guys can't keep your hands off each other. Which, as a divorce attorney, I can tell you is rare. These dreams are not some secret wish fulfillment. They're just dreams."

"Thanks, Rosie. I love you."

Emi knew talking to her sister would help her sort through her feelings. And though she would never admit it out loud, Rose was almost always right. But something she said was already stuck in Emi's chest.

I don't think I can bring myself to unfriend him. At least, not yet.

Even still, Emi lightened, and she breathed a sigh of relief as the sun set with purple clouds behind the tree line. It was anxiety and nothing more. Once she relaxed, life would go on as it was supposed to.

"That screen would have done nothing to save me, by the way."

"I told you that one day, you'd bring me here," Jesse said, eyes twinkling in the dark.

The Eiffel Tower sparkled behind them, and a cold November breeze blew through her hair over the Pont des Arts. Emi lifted her head from Jesse's chest and, wrapped in his warm embrace, looked up into her husband's eyes.

He kissed her in the dim light of the Parisian lamppost. The neurons firing in Emi's head could produce only one thought. This was the most romantic moment of her life. And her heart only felt one thing. That she was with the one soul she was supposed to be with, at the exact place and time that was meant to be.

As she opened her eyes from their kiss and smiled at him, her heart began to drop. The scene's periphery blurred and quickly closed in on them. The bridge, bicycle locks, streetlamp, and finally, Jesse rapidly disappeared into white mist.

Emi clenched him tightly but grew desperate with panic as he slipped out of her grasp into nothingness.

She wrenched awake. Disappointment in herself set in immediately—she'd had another dream. But worse than the letdown was the immense love for Jesse and the fear she was left with when he slipped away. Her heart ached with sorrow.

"Bad dream?" Josh asked, straightening his tie. "Your lip was quivering. I was just about to wake you up."

Emi bit her lip and sat up in bed, hoping he couldn't see the guilt on her face. Sometimes, she felt like Josh could peer into her brain and read her thoughts as clearly as a glass-bottom boat peering into the ocean's great unknown.

"I've gotta run," Josh said. He kissed her head, then lingered in the doorway for a second. "You sure you're okay?"

Emi conjured up a half-hearted smile. "Yes. Have a great day, babe. Call me later."

Josh closed the door behind him, and Emi turned to her phone and touched the screen. A photo of the autumn woods behind the lake house, illuminated with its gorgeous yellows and reds, blinked away, revealing the time.

7:07 a.m.

CHAPTER FIVE

2003

"You like this kid. It's been a minute since I've seen you sprung like this," Fae said with a grin as she chucked a fluffy pink pillow at Emi, who frowned.

"Well, I ruined it, so. I guess it doesn't really matter."

"It can't be that bad, right?"

"Oh, no, Fae. It's pretty bad. We had, like, the best day. With the butterflies, the bridge, and we had so much fun at the bar. You thought Jesse was fun, right?"

"Very fun."

"And he's hot, right?"

"Super."

"And, the worst part is, I think he's actually a nice guy."

"There's your first mistake, Emi. Nice guys don't exist."

"Well, he does. And he's kind. You should have heard him talk about his mom and his sister. When I slept over, he wasn't creepy or pushy. And I just feel so, I don't know, myself around him. Or, like, the best version of myself, you know? I feel beautiful and funny, and smart, and all the things when I'm with him."

"Emi, that's because you are all those things."

Emi ignored Fae's statement and kept going. "But when he tried to kiss me, I was distracted by some stupid bird outside his window and choked. You should have seen it. It was an epic fail."

Emi sulked as she sat on their little couch, carefully painting her nails bright pink. "I just wish I could go back in time and change it." Music videos on the TV droned as the fairy lights twinkled in the living room, and Fae lay upside down on her mom's old armchair, her legs stuck up in the air.

"Oh my God, Em, stop," Fae insisted. "Boys fall all over you every time we leave the house. If I didn't love you so much, it would be really fucking annoying. You're perfect. He will try again, trust me. And if he doesn't, then he's a chooch and not smart enough for you, anyway."

"I doubt it. I just have to, like, let it go." She shrugged. Fretting over a boy like this was new to her and made her feel desperate and uncomfortable. "Can we not talk about Jesse anymore?"

"Done," Fae said. "We need to start pregaming for tonight, anyway. We're supposed to meet the Bates Street girls in a couple of hours."

"Max won't be there, right? I do not want to see him. Honestly, that's the last thing I need."

"Ew, I hope not. If he is, we are running."

Emi put the nail polish down on the windowsill and looked through the glass.

"It's been a week. He has my number. If he were interested, he would have called, right?"

"Ugh, Em. I don't see what's so great about this guy," Fae groaned.

"I know. I don't know what my problem is. I don't even really know him."

Fae sat up assertively. "Your problem is you've left yourself wondering because you're too chicken shit to do anything about the fact that, for whatever reason, you actually like this moron," she said, matter-of-fact. "You've always had your pick and don't know how to put yourself out there. Just go ask him out. I can't take it anymore."

"What would that even look like? I've never asked a guy out." Just the idea freaked Emi out.

"I know, princess," Fae condescended as she patted Emi's head. "It's not that hard, promise. All you do is find a reason to see him again. Didn't you wear his hoodie home?"

Emi nodded, eyes wide, riding Fae's bolt of inspiration.

"So, call him and tell him you're bringing his sweatshirt back. And once you're there, be all, 'Hey, Jesse!'" she purred as she stuck her boobs out and batted her eyelashes. "'What are you doing tonight?' He'll be all over it. Promise. Oh, and make sure to touch him." Fae stroked Emi's arm. "And giggle. Boys love a giggle. They're so dumb."

"Gross. That sounds demeaning."

Fae nodded wisely. "Yep. That's why they like it."

"Yeah, no. I just can't. He's the boy. He's supposed to do it. And he hasn't, which means he doesn't want to."

"Impressive." Fae slow-clapped. "You should teach a master class in fucked-up gender ideology and self-gaslighting. Good thing I picked up a little something to help you chill the eff out."

Fae reached into her purse, pulled out a tiny plastic baggie containing two small pills, and handed one over.

"I'll do it if you do," she teased with a devilish smile.

Emi cocked an eyebrow, intrigued. A dare had been posed. Fae always knew exactly how to trigger her reckless side. And though Emi knew Fae was goading her, she loved it.

"I don't know, Fae. We're not sixteen, rolling all night at some crumbling warehouse rave anymore. I've done enough drugs, I'm kinda over it."

"It's not like I'm asking you to drop acid with me in Frick Park 'til the sun comes up. You've just been so sullen lately, I thought maybe you could use a night of careless fun." Fae paused as her trap was set, then went in for the kill. "I know you want to," she prodded. "Xanax is supposed to be super fun to drink with. Anyway, a doctor prescribed them, so they can't be that bad, right?"

"I'm not sure that's accurate." Emi chuckled and then said, finally. "Okay. We can try it. But let's not make this a regular thing, cool?"

A wide grin stretched across Fae's mouth, and she held up two painted fingers in pledge. Emi followed, and they spoke in unison. "Girl Scout Promise."

"So, are we bumping or swallowing?"

"You know you're a swallower, you little slut," Fae said, grinning at her joke.

"Yeah, yeah, you got me." Emi laughed. Her adrenaline soared as she shared a knowing look with Fae. Adventure awaited, and Emi was ready to ride the party waves wherever they would go.

Emi's consciousness blurred in and out as each sip of her cocktail coincided with the rhythm of club music. Her body was on autopilot; the black box in her mind only recorded fleeting moments, few and far between.

She placed two overflowing shot glasses of tawny liquor on the sticky high-top in front of them. She and Fae promptly plopped them into bigger glasses filled with yellow-orange energy drinks and chugged them as fast as possible.

"I win!" Emi exclaimed as she slammed her empty glass down and raised her hands for the definitive win.

"That's not fair. I wasn't racing!" Fae laughed and wiped her messy face. Emi looked at her with intoxicated gratitude.

"You're my best friend, Fae."

"I know, you're mine, too."

"Thank you for making me come out tonight."

"You needed to blow it out. Sometimes a girl just needs to get really fucking drunk."

Emi nodded sloppily. "Wise words, my friend."

Suddenly, she was in the DJ booth, pouring liquor from a large glass bottle and into the open mouths of the Bates Street girls.

"This is my favorite song!" she yelled as 50 Cent scratched over the loudspeakers. Fae shimmied her way over, doing the running man. She and Emi caught eyes and broke into the choreographed sprinkler dance they had made up as kids, laughing so hard they almost fell over.

The world fizzled and spun, and she, Fae, and Bates Street girls spun with it. Emi shut her eyes and opened them.

Fae now sat haphazardly on the sink counter in the girls' bathroom, consoling Emi while she laughed at herself through her tears.

"It's so stupid, I know."

"Em. Fuck that guy. Jesse sucks."

"I just feel like such an idiot. Like, I don't know why I can't just let it go. He's some kid I literally hung out with like, one time. What's my problem? Oh my God, have I turned into Max?"

"Sweet Jesus, no! But you're right, you haven't been yourself. And I know it's bad because you won't shut up about it." Fae laughed. "It's time to get over this jag-off and remember who you are."

She hugged Emi and wiped the black mascara from under her eyes. Emi turned to the mirror to fix her makeup and then pushed her boobs up under her crop top, taking a deep breath.

"You're right," she said. "If he doesn't like me because of one fucked-up moment, then he's an idiot."

"Yes. Now say it: fuck that guy," Fae prodded.

"Fuck that guy."

Her mind whirled and the bathroom dissolved. Strobe lights shot around the room, casting Emi in a purple light. She was flirting with a kid from high school, but he slipped away from her for a moment, and then Fae was there, propped at the bar where he once stood.

"Can we go home with Dante?" Emi asked her excitedly. "After part-ay!"

Fae gave her a side-eye. "You want to hook up with Dante Apreal?"

"Obviously. And you know we never leave each other, so please can we go? I'm always your wingman, and it's time to be mine," Emi pleaded like a little girl begging for a pony. "Dante's so hot, and he's not some stranger. We know him, so it's fine. Also, he's been trying me for years, so I'd be doing a mitzvah." She nodded vigorously.

"Oh, yeah. You're so charitable," Fae snickered.

Dante slid back over with a Cheshire smile. His chin dimpled with his grin, and his silver chain necklace sparkled in the strobe lights.

"Hey, Fae. Emi and I are just reminiscing."

"Hey, Dante. So I noticed."

"You girls going to come hang out, or what?"

"Uh." Fae looked at Emi, who was swaying slightly, then gave a hiccup. "Sure."

"You need a ride?"

"No," Fae said assertively. "North Oakland, right? I think I remember."

"You sure you're okay to drive?" Dante asked. Fae squinted at him, though her eyes were already half closed from all the downers. Then, all at once, her face lit up, and she shot him a mischievous smile.

"Yep. We will see you there."

Dante reached over, smarmily pulled Emi in by a belt loop, and whispered in her ear. She giggled, but as they sauntered off, leaving him with his friends, a few stray words caught in her ear.

"Emi Fucking Klein," he murmured. "Finally."

Fae's harsh knock on the apartment door snapped Emi out of what felt like a dream.

She had been leaning crookedly against the wall as if she were going to fall asleep standing up like a horse. But the noise of her best friend's fist on the thin wood powered her consciousness back on, and Emi managed to get out half a sentence before it swung open.

"Wait a second, Fae. This isn't Dante's . . ."

And then he was there. Jesse stood in front of them, rubbing sleep out of his eyes. Before Emi could protest, Fae shoved her through the dark doorway.

Emi whipped around.

"I thought we were going to Dante's! What are we doing here?"

But Fae didn't acknowledge her. She simply walked right through the apartment and into the living room as if she had been there a hundred times before. Emi followed closely on her heels, panic bubbling up like vomit.

Matt was cozied up on the couch with three girls, his arm draped over one of them, his smile seeping his sleazy desire. A nitrous tank was to the right of the coffee table, and they were passing a joint around in a circle. Startled, they looked up in glassy-eyed bewilderment at the disheveled newcomers.

Emi grabbed Fae's hand and tugged toward the front door, but Fae snatched it back. She shooed one of the girls and plopped down on the couch, not caring about their intrusion.

"Just talk to him, Emi, Jesus," she slurred, annoyed that Emi wasn't following her plan. Their audience watched raptly as if a live show had stepped out of the TV and into their living room.

"Fae, please. We weren't invited. We shouldn't be here," Emi implored.

"Emelie Collette Klein. We can't leave now. I'm too fucked up. I drove with one eye shut all the way from Oakland. If I try to drive again, we will die. Please, just talk to Jesse and get it over with so we can all go to bed."

And with that, Fae got up, huffed around for the bedroom, and collapsed in a heap onto the first mattress she found.

Alone without Fae, Emi suddenly grasped the stares gawking in her direction. Her head spun with liquor and sedatives, and her blood pumped fast and heavy with panic.

I have to get out of here.

Without a word, she stood and passed Jesse in the doorway, unable to look him in the face. Emi pulled out her phone and dialed a number, ignoring the laughter at her expense from the living room. She didn't know or give a shit about those people or what they thought of her.

But she did care about Jesse. She hated that she cared so much.

Though her phone call had only been a couple of minutes, she found Fae out like a light on Jesse's bed.

"Fae. Fae, wake up, it's time to leave. Fae, please!" Emi shook her desperately. "Lydia lives two blocks away. She's on her way to meet us. Come on, Fae, please!"

"Um, I have to work in the morning. Are you staying the night, or what's happening?" Jesse asked as he stepped into his room, clearly annoyed.

"No," Emi said, meeting his eyes for the first time. "Our friend is coming to get us. I'm really sorry. I know we just, like, barged in on you. I still don't know why we're here."

"Emi, please, I'm so tired," Fae groaned, half unconscious. "Just leave me."

"It's cool. You girls can stay over, but you have to go to sleep now. It's like three in the morning, and I have to wake up in four hours," Jesse said, a little more forcefully this time. Emi recoiled as humiliation stabbed through her drunken heart.

She woke up on the couch, her mouth arid and her skin damp with cold sweat that smelled like cheap liquor. A blanket had been draped over her, and her feet ached from the shoes she had slept in. Emi could feel the layer of smeared makeup sinking into her pores and looked down at her purse spewed out beneath her on the floor.

The afternoon light streamed through the white curtains, and a glass of water with two ibuprofen waited patiently for her on the coffee table. Emi sat up and looked around.

Where am I?

It took a moment for her to realize she was in Lydia's apartment. Her head pounded as she tried to recall how she got there.

Oh, shit.

Dread settled in the pit of her stomach. It had been a while since she had that awful, looming, anxious feeling—the realization she'd blacked out and done something embarrassing. She hated not being able to remember what she would have to apologize for.

Emi scanned the living room for signs of Fae and remembered that she had left her friend behind.

"Oh. My. God." Flashes from the night before came back to her and played in her mind like a bad dream. She cradled her head in her hands as her breathing became shallow.

Lydia walked in, still in her pj's and holding two cups of coffee. She handed one to Emi, who cringed.

"Girl, what happened last night?" she asked worriedly. "All I could get out of you was that you were somewhere you shouldn't have been."

"Lydia, I am such an asshole. Well, he definitely thinks I'm fucking crazy now." Emi checked her cell, but it was dead. "Can I use your phone to call Fae? I can't believe I left her there last night, and I need to make sure she's okay."

"She's fine. She called me an hour ago. I told her I'd bring you home. Now, what guy? What the hell happened?"

A few hours later, Emi stepped out of the steamy shower, finally clean from washing off her humiliation and feeling a little better. Fae was lying on her bed, flipping through a magazine.

"That Pacey can get it," Fae said. "He is so hot. I can't even." She looked up as Emi sat next to her, one towel in her hair, one wrapped around her body.

"Well, Jesse thinks I'm a fucking psycho. And I can't even imagine what Matt thought of our little production. Why the hell were we there? I thought I was supposed to hook up with Dante?"

"You were. But I took you to Jesse's instead," Fae said sheepishly. "I just thought if the two of you stopped this dumb little dance, you guys would admit that you both like each other and get on with it. I'm sorry. It's all my fault."

"It's okay, Fae. It was a good idea, in theory. I'm sure I could have handled it better, too."

"Ain't that the truth," Fae said with a smile. "I guess I figured if you were too chicken shit to put yourself out there, then I would do it for you. But maybe it would have been better if you met up another time. Maybe a more sober time."

"Ya think?"

"Yeah, well. I maintain he's a fucking idiot. But you were right—he is actually a nice guy. And they were totally cool with me staying there, even after we busted in on them in the middle of the night."

Swallowing the public mortification and defeat, Emi resigned herself to just being sad.

"But he's still a jerk-off. Because blacked out or not, you're perfect, and he doesn't get that, so I hate him forever. Listen. The semester's almost over. And they're all going to go back to wherever they came from. If it's really done, like you think, then let's take your power back. What if we put his phone number in the prank call rotation? We can at least have some fun with it."

Emi hesitated but stood up with a resigned sigh and threw her phone on the bed.

"Here, have at it. But please delete him from my phone when you're done. And leave me out of it."

"Done," Fae said as she picked up Emi's phone and searched through the contacts. "Fuck that guy," she muttered. "He doesn't know what he's in for. Now, you want to hear something really funny?"

"Yes, please. Anything to change the subject."

"Hit play on the voicemail in the kitchen. Dante left, like, six messages last night wondering where you were."

"Oh my God, stop!"

"Hey, girl! I've missed you. Get over here . . ."

Lydia gave Emi an excited squeeze on the SAE frat house's front porch. College kids were stuffed into the old, crumbly row house, spilling out onto the lawn. Some even sat on the pitched roof, rap music thumping out of every window. Nothing said summer to Emi more than red plastic cups and flip-flops.

"I've missed you too," Emi answered, her silver hoop earrings shining in the early moonlight. "I just got back a couple of days ago."

"Was Spain just, like, everything? Look at your tan, girl. Oh my God, I'm so jealous."

"Thanks! A month on the Mediterranean will do it."

"So, do you get to travel at the end of every semester?"

"Yeah, pretty much. My parents usually go somewhere over the break, so Rose and I try to meet up with them for a bit, wherever they are."

Fae bounded over with a cup in each hand, like a puppy with a ball. But as she handed one to Emi, a look of reservation painted her face.

"So, um. Matt is here," she said as she nodded toward the house. Emi's face dropped.

But she could feel in her bones Jesse wasn't with him.

"I didn't see Jesse, though," Fae quickly added, validating her instinct. Just the thought of Jesse smacked Emi with a triple whammy of emotions. First came relief that she wouldn't have to face him, then embarrassment and melancholy.

"Jesse's the guy from the apartment, right?" Lydia chimed in. But Emi couldn't focus on her right now.

"Did Matt see you?" she asked Fae.

"Yeah. I didn't realize it was him until it was too late, so I apologized for showing up uninvited and causing drama, or whatever."

Emi swallowed hard. "Was he nice about it?"

"Yeah, I was surprised, but he was chill about it."

"That's good, I guess. I should probably apologize, too . . ."

"Or we could just leave," Fae said. "You don't need to do anything. It was my fault. I'm the one who took us there."

"No. I should apologize. That's, like, the right thing to do."

"You want me to come with you?" Fae asked. Emi shook her head.

"I'm a big girl. I'm just going to get it over with. Where is he?"

"In the backyard, by the keg."

Matt was right where Fae said he would be, sitting on a rusty metal gliding chair, surrounded by a group of people she didn't know. Emi wondered if they were the same girls who had been at his apartment a few weeks ago. They certainly could have been. She had no clue. Though Emi had mustered up enough courage to apologize, she hadn't thought through what exactly she would say.

"Hey," she began. Emi felt so foolish, like a jester in front of the king and his court.

Suddenly, she was hyperaware of her hands and what to do with them. Fae told her he would be amiable, but Matt looked at her with searing contempt. Emi shifted her weight from one foot to the other, confused and unprepared for the intensity of his disdain.

"Can I talk to you for a second?" she asked politely. Matt rolled his eyes before making a show of getting up. They stepped a few feet away and stood next to the ivy-covered fence. He crossed his arms and pouted, making it clear he wouldn't be easy on her.

"Fae told me you were here. I just wanted to say I'm sorry. You know, for making a scene at your apartment. Especially when we weren't invited." He pursed his lips but didn't say anything, so she nervously rambled on. "We were so drunk we hardly remember. That's not an excuse, but, you know, for some context. We're usually not like that. Anyway, I'm super embarrassed."

Finally, Emi forced herself to stop talking and wait for a response.

"Well. You should be embarrassed," Matt sneered coldly.

Emi didn't know what she had expected, but it wasn't that. Maybe, *"It's fine, we're all ridiculous sometimes,"* or *"Don't worry about it, it wasn't that bad."* But for some reason, this dude had a hard-on for her and made it plain he would be the opposite of understanding.

She winced inside and turned to leave, having said all she could.

"I knew you were shady," Matt said dismissively. Emi could feel her whole demeanor change and whipped back around.

"What?" Now, she was the indignant one. "I may be a lot of things, but shady is not one of them."

"Did you know I'm friends with Max? I just think it's fucked up that you're dating him and messing with Jesse's head at the same time. Jesse really liked you, and you were playing him," he seethed. "I told him, you know, that you had a boyfriend. I know a lot of girls like you. You all think you're so hot that you can do whatever you want. But you can't. Jesse's my best friend, and he's been hurt before. I'm not going to let you walk all over him."

"You don't know me at all." Emi was visibly shaking. "I don't care what you think you know or what Max told you about me. I ended it with him weeks before I even met Jesse. Maybe you'll get your information straight before you meddle in his life next time."

"Whatever," he scoffed. "I'm just looking out. You know, bro code."

"That's the dumbest shit I have ever heard. Bro code?" Emi laughed maniacally at the ridiculousness of it all.

But something changed in Matt's eyes. His expression went limp as his fuel began to peter.

"Okay, well. If you weren't with Max, then I am actually sorry," he said. "Maybe I shouldn't have gotten involved. But I was just being a friend."

"Some friend." Emi looked around the party. "Is Jesse here?"

"Ah, nah. He's in Rochester for the summer. He's going to Cornell for grad school, so I doubt he'll be back," Matt said smugly.

Emi's heart plunged.

He decided to go.

"Good for him," she said, faking a smile.

She snaked her way back through the party, shell-shocked.

At least it's over.

She had liked this kid whom she hardly knew more than maybe anyone ever. But for various reasons, both in and out of her control, it just hadn't worked out. She would never have a chance to redeem herself or even explain, so it was time to let it go.

As Emi slipped through the crowd she swore to herself, *I will never speak of Jesse Amato, ever again.*

CHAPTER SIX

2005

The end of winter in western Pennsylvania always meant one more good old-fashioned snowstorm. Which invariably showed up uninvited, like a jealous ex, on Emi's birthday, coming in hot to ruin the fun.

This year was no different. Snow fell silently like round, fluffy cotton balls. It blanketed the hushed city under its majestic spell, which was beautiful but made for a precarious situation. Roads were slicked over, and the metal of snowplows rumbled past establishments as they prepared for the night's festivities, kicking off the holiday weekend and annual Saint Patrick's Day parade the next morning.

Emi's neon green high heels were slipping and sliding all over the pavement as she carefully shuffled down Walnut Street. The green, blinking feather boa her friends had given her for the night was itching already. But she didn't care. It was her twenty-third birthday. And she and four of her best girlfriends were shivering their way through the yuppie district of Shadyside in tiny skirts and green crop tops, arms linked in a futile attempt at warmth.

The door to Doc's Saloon shone like a mirage at the end of the block. They had almost made it unscathed until something stopped them in their tracks.

Someone was standing before the ATM in front of the bar.

Someone Emi hadn't seen for a long time.

A warm voice, sweet and familiar like a daydream, filled the air between them as the would-be stranger turned around. "Emi?"

"Oh my God, Josh? Josh Felice?" Fae gasped in delight. "How are you? We haven't seen you in forever," she said as she threw her arms around him. "Look at you, all handsome and shit."

Josh was cute. He was tall and lean with the same easy smile and familiar, amber eyes as always, but his features were older now and more manly.

"I'm good. How are you?" he echoed, hugging Fae back but smiling at Emi, who stood behind her. "Emi, you look amazing. You both do."

He hugged her next, and she signaled the rest of the girls to stop their teeth chattering and head into the bar.

Emi smiled. "What's it been? Ten years, maybe?"

Excitement tickled Emi's insides as the wind kicked up the snow around them, and for a second or two, it was just the two of them in their own enchanted snow globe. Far-off whispers swirled something in her ear. And from the look in his eye, she was sure he heard it, too. Fae's voice brought them back to earth. "How's your sister? I haven't seen her since graduation."

"Oh, uh. She's good. She's at Virginia Tech for her master's."

His gaze stayed on Emi as he nodded at the bar behind them. "I'm meeting some friends here. Let me buy you a drink. You are old enough now, right?" he teased.

"Uh, yes, dummy. And make it two, because it's my birthday!"

Two-thirty a.m. came too quickly as a crowd of drunk and hungry partygoers swarmed the pizza place at the far end of the street. It was a tradition for anyone drinking on Walnut Street to end up at Village Pizza to cap off their night.

"Alright. You ready? We gotta go get our stuff and head out," Greg, Josh's best friend, said after finishing off his third slice of pepperoni.

Josh deflated and stole a glance at Emi across the table. He turned to his buddy, who was looking expectantly at him, and only then did Emi realize all four of his friends were giving him the same impatient look.

"Shouldn't we leave in the morning? It's pretty late," Josh tried, shooting Greg pleading eyes. Emi tried her best not to let a grin eat her face.

"Where are you guys going?" Fae asked.

"We're driving to Indianapolis for March Madness."

"What?" The girls put their pizza down in surprise.

"We've been slamming shots for, like, four and a half hours." Emi laughed. "You shouldn't even be driving down the block."

"Well," Josh mumbled, "we were supposed to leave earlier, but . . ."

"Famous last words," Fae sighed.

"Emi, can I get your number?" Josh blurted. It must've come out louder than he meant because a hush settled, and every set of eyes in the hole-in-the-wall restaurant seemed to fall upon them.

"I guess so," she said after making a show of considering him.

Drunken cheers and a round of applause broke out from the bystanders, and Josh pulled her hand to stand up. He bowed as she blushed and gave a curtsey to their unintended audience.

"So, when can I call you?" he asked in her ear.

"Maybe when you get back from Indianapolis."

"With those knuckleheads driving, it's more like if I get back."

Emi stood on an old iron balcony, watching dark green waves crash across a mustard-colored beach. She hung up the phone and walked back into the tiny oceanside room with two damp, salty beds, dingy yellow walls, drab red carpeting, and crooked blinds that hadn't been dusted since the seventies. But it overlooked the busy boardwalk, so the dank covers and faint smell of mold and cigarette smoke were worth it.

Fae looked up at Emi expectantly and smiled. She was pretending to primp for their night out, but Emi could tell by the look on her face she had been eavesdropping.

"So, how's Joshy?"

"He's good. He asked if we wanted to leave Jersey a day or two early and head up to Connecticut to spend a few days at his parents' island house," Emi said casually.

"Damn, Em, I knew he was rich, but I didn't know he was *island* rich."

"I think they inherited it or something. And it's not Josh's island. It's his parents'."

"Old money is so hot."

Emi rolled her eyes. "I really don't care about his money."

"Well, I do. Anyway, it's been months. Are you stringing this poor boy along, or what?"

"I don't know. Anyway, do you want to go? Greg is there, too, so we would two-man it."

"Oh my God, Sexy Greg? I'm in. And we still have four hundred and thirty-two dollars left. Go us," Fae said as she counted their money stash and then hid it again in a box of tampons in her oversized duffle bag.

"I say we grab some pizza and then meet up with those cute guys next door. You know the tall one likes you," Fae fished. Emi ignored the bait. "Maybe I can borrow your denim miniskirt, oh, and your trucker hat."

"You should definitely wear my skirt. And the hat is in my bag. I'll wear my new tube top," Emi offered, sitting crisscross on her bed with her makeup mirror held up to her face as she started in on her eyeliner. "And yeah, those boys are fun. But I'm not really interested. I'm happy just hanging out."

Fae eyed Emi skeptically from across the room.

Emi sighed.

"I like Josh, I do. I just. I don't know. I guess I'm taking it slowly, you know?"

"I don't get it. He's cute. He has, like, ambitions and a career path. He's rich as fuck, and he really likes you. Plus, you said the sex is fire. What's the hold-up?"

"You're right. He's perfect, but . . ." Her voice softened; she was struggling. "Maybe too perfect. He's almost a real adult with a respectable job and a savings account. I always date stoner guys that seem to be stuck in college."

"I'm not seeing the problem here."

"He's never done drugs. Like, ever. Maybe smoked weed freshman year, but that's it. And it's not like I want to anymore, either. But, like, we were wild in high school. We snuck out of the house constantly and ran away from cops at keg parties. We would trip on acid or shrooms until the sun came up and dated guys who were way too old for us. We have a range of friends, from drug dealers to premed. Some of them being the same people."

Then there's Josh, who stole street signs when he wanted to be bad. His parents adore him. He is the definition of a golden child. He's never had a friend die, much less of an overdose. In fact, I'm not sure anything seedy has ever happened to Josh, like, ever. He hasn't had experiences like I have. Everything's come easily for him. He's like that Beaver kid from the fifties."

"He's too vanilla for you, is that it? Maybe some stability and a normal guy would be good for a change," Fae said.

"Yeah, maybe. Those are some of the things I like about him, but they scare me, too. Sometimes I wonder if we are just so different that he won't get me, you know? Maybe I'm too much for him. Maybe he's too tame for me. Plus, he's older than us, and I think he might want something more serious."

It was half the truth. Emi *knew* Josh wanted more because a week ago—when she'd left for vacation—he'd asked her for it. He wanted more than just hangouts and sex. She promised to think about it, but he was waiting for an answer, and a part of Emi feared this was the reason for his impromptu invitation.

"Okay, like, how serious?"

"It's not just that, Fae. I'm also worried that he won't live up to my expectations. Maybe whatever is between us—though it's great—isn't what I think love should be."

Fae looked befuddled. "What do you think it should be?"

"I don't know," Emi said dreamily. "The all-consuming, stars-exploding, worlds-colliding, I-can't-live-without-you, soulmate kind of love?"

"Emelie Klein," Fae said with a widening grin. "Since when did you become such a romantic?"

Emi threw a sandy pillow at her friend.

"Okay, okay." Fae snickered. "So, you're looking for the love of your life, and you don't think Josh is it. That's fair."

"But maybe he could be. Things feel so right and safe with him. I sleep better next to him than ever in my life. It's like he calms my nervous system. But then I get all up in my head about it and freak myself out."

"Well, he's completely obsessed with you. That's obvious." Emi looked up from her makeup mirror again. "Oh, come on, Em. You know it was love at first sight for him, everyone could see it. When he saw you on that street corner, it was like nobody else even existed. It's cute how he looks at you all googly-eyed. I wish someone looked at me like that."

Emi fell silent as she slipped into her thoughts.

Do I even believe in love at first sight?

She had only felt lightning strike once before, but it couldn't have been anything special because nothing had come of it. Emi pushed any thought that might lead to Jesse Amato out of her head as quickly as it had popped in.

"I'm just not sure I'm ready for a big commitment, I guess," Emi admitted, hoping this would end the conversation and they could get back to primping in earnest.

"How will you ever know if he's your supernova, worlds-colliding, whatever-whatever kind of love if you don't give him a real chance?" Fae asked, digging through her duffle bag and throwing things out while looking for her other flip-flop.

"Why are you so annoying?" Emi huffed. "Fine. We will visit Josh and Greg in Connecticut for a day or two, and I'll see how it goes. Happy?"

"Actually, yes," Fae said with a satisfied look. "And I'm going to have island sex with Hot Greg."

CHAPTER SEVEN

Emi pulled her car up to the dock and looked out on the water.

"This is the place?" she asked.

Fae double-checked the road map and shuffled through the three pages of directions she printed at the front desk of their motel.

"I think so. He said three o'clock?"

Emi nodded and looked at her cell phone. No missed calls.

They searched the water in silence for just a few moments before the familiar sounds of a motorboat approached.

The calm waters began to shift, turning to waves. Then, steering from the back of a small boat, sun-kissed and windswept, Josh appeared. Emi's stomach flipped in excitement and relief. It was at this moment she realized that she had missed him. And if she missed him, then her feelings for him were real.

Josh stealthily pulled up to the dock and reached his hand out to help Emi onto the boat. She couldn't tell if it was the sun bouncing off the water or if it was Josh, but light shone so brightly in her eyes that she had to squint. Smiling like a schoolboy, he brought her in for a kiss on her bronzed cheek.

"I'm glad you made it," he said in her ear. Emi blushed, and Josh moved on to help Fae board.

The water further from the mainland was choppy, and Emi and Fae bumped up and down in the little boat. At last, they came to a small island capped with huge green maples glowing brightly in the summer sun. A yellow two-story estate with a wraparound porch and a nautical-blue front door grew out of the tree line and into view.

As they motored closer, Emi noticed a hammock strung between two tall trees, and goosebumps crept up her body. Suddenly, a recurring childhood dream came to her like an unsolvable riddle.

A little girl with pigtails and large amber eyes lay snuggled in Emi's arms, and they laughed easy and free as someone pushed them gently, swinging in the hammock. Ocean breeze swept through the holes of the rope, and a seabird flapped its wings nearby. The girl reached her pudgy arms up and stuck her doll-sized fingers in Emi's hair, twisting it around her fingertips.

Emi blinked herself back as they pulled up to the dock and parked the boat next to a sign that read *Bluebird Landing*. Josh strung up the boat and hopped out, extending his hand to help the girls once again.

They walked through the meticulously manicured yard, up the polished wood stairs, and into the house, which was as warm and inviting inside as it was on the outside. Tall ceilings and thick molding greeted them in the foyer, and a large stone fireplace stood elegantly in the living room.

Their stay in the enclave was a midsummer night's dream, with fireflies dancing in the trees. They could have been the only souls left on the planet. Laughter bounced off the water as they drank IPAs around the firepit, lounged in deep Adirondack chairs, and watched the sun set fire to the early July sky.

Stars twinkled serendipitously as Emi and Josh left their friends for the privacy of the hot tub. Moonbeams bouncing in their eyes, they lost themselves in each other. Hazy and passionate sex flowed with the steamy water bubbling like a love potion around their bodies as they took over.

In some strange way, as if she'd connected to the drifting cosmos that swirled above, Emi could feel she was exactly where she was meant to be—in that hot tub, on that private isle, in the middle of the Connecticut waters, with Josh Felice.

She rolled over to an empty bed, and late-morning light streamed through tall curtains.

It was July seventh, and she and Fae would have to leave the day after next. Pulling herself up and swinging her feet to the floor, Emi noticed a large cup of coffee and a note on the bedside table.

Latte with two sugars, the way you like. Went for a walk, enjoy the quiet – J

She brushed her teeth, threw on a pair of Josh's plaid boxer shorts, and carried her coffee outside, finding a good seat on the shady side of the dock. She dangled her legs over the edge and cracked open her favorite book but found herself mesmerized by the calm ripples of the water, lost in her thoughts.

Emi knew Josh was falling in love with her, though he didn't say it. She could feel it in his stare when he thought she wasn't looking and in his arms when he held her at night. She knew he would want her to make her feelings clear—soon.

A cool breeze picked up, and she watched the oak leaves rustle in the wind above her. Then, inexplicably, Emi's mind fell under the shadow of a memory she could not remember.

Old, towering pines stretched to the sky in a half circle around a meadow of tall grass and wildflowers.

Just as quickly as it had come, her vision flashed back to the dock. Before she could even begin to think about what she had just seen, much less dismiss it as imagination, Emi's eyes flooded with tears.

Was she really holding back with Josh because he was a golden boy who was too good for her, or didn't meet her expectations of what love should feel like? Or was she hiding behind excuses because she didn't want to admit the true problem?

Though it had been years, and she'd had many boyfriends since, Emi had never gotten over that one guy.

That one, stupid guy.

The one she never kissed, slept with, or even got to know. She didn't know his middle name or his favorite movie. But she had felt a certain way about him, in just one day, that she never felt again.

And the idea that she might be devoid of that feeling forever terrified her.

But she couldn't hold on to Jesse Amato anymore because of something that just hadn't been. Whatever happened between them meant nothing because it was nothing. Josh, however, was everything. And it was time to let go of what wasn't and embrace what was.

The sun poked out from behind a cloud as she closed her eyes. Emi wiped the streams of tears from her face and made up her mind.

Okay, I'm all in with Josh.

The rustling sound of feathers close by startled her, and Emi's heart skipped a beat as she suddenly found herself three feet from a large blue crane. It looked her straight in the eyes, picked up out of the water, and flew right over her head—close enough that she could feel the wind under its wings on her face, brushing the hair off her shoulders. It soared away with only two full flaps and disappeared as quickly as it had come.

Jesse

The speedboat pulled a fast turn and came to an abrupt stop, large waves catching up and splashing high on its sides. A crew of twenty-somethings in bathing suits nodded and rapped along to the lyrics blasting off a pocket-size MP3 player.

Jesse turned his baseball hat backward, slid on his favorite aviator sunglasses, opened the cooler, and began tossing cold beers to his friends. Matt threw an innertube into the water.

"Hey, birthday boy, you up first?"

Jesse shook his head. "Nah, not yet. I'm going to have a beer or two and work on my tan," he joked.

Matt turned to a blond girl in a tiny bikini. She giggled, stood up, and began lowering herself into the tube from the back of the boat.

As everyone was preoccupied with the mostly naked girl twisting herself to get into the raft without losing her top, Jesse noticed something standing tall in the shade, under the trees, by the shore.

A four-foot blue crane was looking directly at him. They stared each other in the eye for several seconds before it suddenly picked up from the marsh, flapped its enormous wings once or twice, and soared gracefully right over him. It had been close enough that he almost reached up and touched it.

The boat collectively gasped.

"Whoa! That was so cool!" the girl blurted from her innertube, paddling her arms excitedly over the water. "Did you see how big that was?"

Jesse watched quietly, a chill running up his spine. A strange, achy feeling spread over him as the bird flew out of sight.

CHAPTER EIGHT

2022

Stella trotted happily on the cool, damp pavement. A summer storm had brought a chill to Aspen, which was her favorite weather for a walk. Her spotted beagle tail whipped back and forth like a window wiper as she looked up, tongue wagging.

Jesse wasn't feeling so perky. He was ambivalent about being stateside again. Having spent the last three weeks traipsing around the Mediterranean, he had come home to find a pit in his stomach and an old depression waiting for him.

He had the career he had always dreamt of. He had a great dog, a beautiful home, and lots of friends and family. Life was still a party. But the more he had, with nobody to share it with, the lonelier he became.

Maybe committing to one person for the rest of my life just isn't for me.

He had told himself this every time he broke up with someone. And for many years, it was true. But the words were hollow now. Something big, something meaningful, felt like it had changed in him.

Once they reached the park, Jesse let Stella off her leash and watched like a proud dad as she frolicked with a pack of rowdy, mismatched dogs. He found a bench in the shade, pulled his phone out of his hoodie, and sighed.

She hasn't responded.

Emi had left their chat and his last casual message with just a heart.

It was great to run into you. Maybe we will meet again someday.

Jesse cringed at the cliché more and more every time he read it. He wondered if she thought it sounded as stupid as he did. Maybe if he really tried, he could will her to write back.

He was deep in this thought when a flash of color caught his eye.

A bluebird shot from the woods and darted up to him as if it had an urgent message. Stunned, Jesse watched on as it stopped short, suspended in midair, and flapped its wings at him for three full seconds. Then it simply turned and took off in the opposite direction as if nothing curious had happened, leaving him open-mouthed.

He looked around to see if anyone else had witnessed the anomaly that presented itself to him, but nobody even glanced his way. Jesse shook it off.

Jesus, I'm really losing it. Maybe Jenna is right; I need more sleep.

He checked his phone and called Stella to head back. It was time to get showered up for yet another blind date.

She was a different kind of pretty than the bombshells he usually found himself with. She was more sophisticated, with auburn hair and gray eyes. But though this one seemed smart, she had a haughty look that made Jesse uncomfortable.

"So, you're in graduate school?" Jesse asked and took a sip of his IPA.

"Yeah, political science."

A memory struck him, and for a moment, he was a million miles from his barstool.

Emi's voice whispered in his mind from long ago. *"My mom's an anthropology professor at Pitt, and my dad is dean of their political science department."*

He winced.

Stop it, Jesse.

He wished it was Emi's face sitting across the table, and for a moment, her big brown eyes smiled back at him from the other side of his beer. He blinked. She was gone, and his date was back.

Don't think about Emi, don't think about Emi. God damn it, what is wrong with me?

She soured as her phone lit up on the table. Obviously perturbed, she picked it up, typed furiously, and then set it down with a dramatic thunk.

"What are you planning on doing after you graduate? Do you want to go into—"

Her phone lit up again. This time, she rolled her eyes and huffed, pursed her lips, and held a flippant finger up to tell him to wait.

Jesse tried not to sound annoyed. "Is it important? I can give you a minute if you need."

"No," she said. "I'm so done with him."

"Okay, no problem. So, I was asking if you wanted to get into politics or teach after—"

But an incoming call cut him off again, reverberating their drinks as it buzzed furiously.

"What?" she snapped as she answered. Jesse got up from the table to excuse himself but didn't get two feet before he heard her start to argue.

"Well, you're the one who said we should see other people. I don't know, some guy. Aren't you out with Little Miss BBL? No. Anyway, he's not really my type. Plus, he's like forty."

Ouch.

Jesse sighed in defeat and strode through the bathroom door, hoping that when he got back, she would be gone.

"I'll be back in a few weeks for your first baseball game, buddy. I wouldn't miss it," Jesse said into his phone as he walked through the parking lot back to his car. "Can I talk to your mom? Love you, too."

It was a hazy afternoon, and the low-lying clouds covered the picturesque Colorado mountain range behind him.

"What's up, Jess? How was the date?" his sister's voice asked through the speaker.

"Hey Jenna. Well, it wasn't great. For starters, she doesn't know who Kurt Cobain was and has barely heard of Biggie."

"A capital offense," she chided.

"Second, I'm pretty sure she's getting back together with an ex as we speak, and third, she made fun of my age. So, I wouldn't start planning the wedding just yet.

But I'm calling because, and don't argue with me, I'm wiring you a gift, and I just need you to know it's coming. Let's just call it an early birthday present."

"Jesse, no. I hate it when you send me money out of the blue."

"Come on, I said don't argue with me. It's not an imposition; don't say that. The market's been hot lately. What good does being rich do if you can't share it with people you love? And you and Caleb are my people. Anyway, be good, little sister. I'll see you in a few days. Love you."

He caught a glimpse of his dark eyes in the rearview mirror, pressed the button to turn on his car, and turned the music up. Just as thick raindrops began to splatter on the windshield, his phone rang over the loudspeaker.

"Hello?"

"Hi, is this Jesse Amato?" a woman's voice asked.

"Yes."

"This is Emilie," she said. Her words kicked the wind out of his lungs. *Holy shit.*

"I'm sorry, who is this?" he asked in disbelief.

"Elodie. From Puppy Palace." Jesse breathed out as his heart sank. "Don't worry, Stella is fine. I'm just calling to let you know she's due for her annual distemper vaccine. We can't board her next week without it. Would you like us to go ahead and give it to her now? We can do it before you pick her up from daycare today."

"Oh, uh, yeah, sure. Thanks for calling."

Jesse's car rolled to a gentle stop at a red light, his mind so far away it could have been in a different dimension. Unable to stop his hands, like a marionette controlled by some other force, he picked up his phone and began typing.

I'll be in town next week. Want to get together?

Emi

The sun warmed her shoulders, and the ends of her shiny hair tickled her back. The street was lined with knotted maple trees as old as the turn-of-the-century buildings they shaded. People strode lackadaisically from one carefully restored hipster storefront to the next, sipping their seven-dollar lattes with Saturday ease.

Emi smiled to herself. She loved Pittsburgh in the summer. The warm air always transported her back to carefree nights with Josh when they were young, and it was just the two of them.

Yogis were out with the last of the morning sun for their weekly group stretch in the park. Granola moms towed overpriced canvas bags, waiting to be filled with organic eggs and artisanal jam before the farmer's market disappeared. The younger brunch crowd was pulling itself out of hangovers and into the daylight, donning their standard weekend uniform of oversized sunglasses and messy topknots that promised giggles, gossip, and bottomless mimosas.

Emi was out for the same, on her way to meet girlfriends, when a pair of gorgeous wedges caught her eye in the shoe store's window. As she peered through the glass to admire them, someone close behind moved toward her in the reflection, and with him came a deep voice.

"Emi?"

Every hair on her body stood at attention as a serendipitous chill tingled up her spine. Holding her breath, she could feel someone else's on her skin. Slowly, Emi turned around.

But there was nobody there.

Perplexed, she looked up and down the street. Though people were bustling by, walking their dogs and talking on their cell phones, she could get no sense of who had spoken to her.

I must have heard a snippet of somebody else's conversation. My name is common enough, she thought, stuffing down the proliferating peculiarity.

As she moved toward the restaurant, though, a warm gush of wind stopped her, brushing the hair off her shoulders. She closed her eyes and breathed in the familiar smell of evergreen.

It reminded her of something, like a memory buried in the back of her brain that was just out of reach. A vision crossed her sight: tattooed hands and their strong fingers interlaced with her own, with a simple, silver, man's wedding ring.

Emi's phone buzzed in her purse, bringing her back to reality. She pulled it out, trembling, as she already knew what it was.

I'll be in town next week. Want to get together?

The exposed brick-and-beam restaurant where her friends met for brunch once a month was one of her favorites. The walls hummed with laughter and clinking silverware over crème fraiche French toast and hand-crafted Bloody Marys. Gen Z and Millennial anecdotes collided over every table, ranging from drunken shenanigans to the most social media-worthy tropical beach vacations, tips on which filter was the best for new babies, and the hottest neighborhoods to buy into.

Emi's friends stood to leave. One after the next, they hugged each other over a mess of half-eaten charcuterie, chocolate mousse cake, and an empty pitcher of sangria. They started their march to the door in single file, but Lauren seemed to be lingering purposefully.

Emi watched on as she kissed Fae goodbye and juggled her purse over her shoulder, but some hesitation appeared to hold her back. Finally, Lauren turned to Emi and laid a hand on her arm.

"Hey, are you okay?"

Caught off guard and a little slow from the drinks, Emi stammered. "Totally. Oh my God, yeah, I'm fine. Why?"

"No reason. You just seem a little, um, distracted lately."

"Oh. I'm sorry. I . . . you know . . . Liam hasn't been sleeping well, and I'm just exhausted."

"Yeah, girl. It's hard to go back once you're used to sleeping through the night again. Tell Josh to let you take a nap. Call me later. Love you!"

"What was that about?" Fae asked as she watched Lauren slip through the door and retreat to her car.

"I'm not sure," Emi said, fighting the uneasy feeling in her stomach that had nothing to do with her mimosa. "She said I seem distracted?"

"Are you?"

"Well, maybe a little."

"Mom has the girls, so I don't have to be home at any particular time. Do you want to grab a coffee? You can tell me what's up."

"Sure, but there's nothing up."

Fae gave her an animated side-eye.

They found an empty table at the café nearby, and Emi looked out of the open garage-door wall and into the beautiful afternoon. She sipped her iced latte.

"So, like . . ." Fae's eyes glistened as she honed in. "Lay it on me."

"It's nothing. Really." But as Fae made a face doused in skepticism, Emi sighed and conceded. "I think I might be having a mental health crisis."

"Uh, I talk to you every day, and you seem pretty healthy to me."

"Fae, I'm serious. The weirdest shit has been happening to me lately, and it's freaking me out. I don't know how to explain it without sounding absolutely insane."

"Try me."

"Today, on the way to brunch, I walked past the little shoe store, and I was looking through the window at these super cute wedges . . . and somebody said my name. Or at least, I could have sworn somebody said my name, but nobody was there when I turned around. I keep seeing the same letters and numbers over and over again. On license plates, billboards, and even on our tab today at brunch. You think I'm crazy."

Fae, who had been listening intently, shook her head.

"No, I don't." She rattled the ice in her coffee. "Let's talk this out. Who do you think visited you? Is it anyone in particular, like an angel or a spirit guide or something?"

"I don't know." She shrugged. "But they felt familiar somehow."

"Okay. What letters are you seeing?"

At this, Emi took a deep breath. "J-A," she answered sheepishly, unable to look up from her lap. "Sometimes E-J-A."

"God, I really hate that dude," Fae said, inferring correctly and shaking her head. "You know, years ago, I thought maybe," she said, more to herself than to Emi, "I was so happy when it turned out to be Josh. But now"—Fae sighed—"I'm not so sure. Fucking Jesse." She huffed in disappointment. "Dare I even ask about the numbers?"

"I keep seeing seven-seven. I think it could be his birthday. I've thought about it and I'm pretty sure he told me it was July seventh."

"Figures." Fae gave an eye roll. "But my feelings aside, let's put this together. You literally bumped into this guy out of nowhere twenty years later. Since then, you've been seeing numbers that coincide with his date of birth and letters of his initials, and now he's astral projecting himself to you."

"Hold up, did you say he astral projected himself?" Emi giggled. "That is not a thing, Fae."

"Yes, it absolutely is. Space and time aren't real. They're just a construct of our tiny, unimaginative, incapable brains. Don't laugh, I am so serious."

"I know you are. But the thought that someone could send their soul to me is, honestly, ridiculous."

"All right, well, we can debate the laws of physics and general relativity later. So, now that we know all of this, what are you going to do?"

"What do you mean?" Emi asked.

"Clearly, there's something happening there. Don't you think you should find out what it is?"

"And how would I do that?"

"I don't know, maybe meet up with him next time he's visiting?"

"Funny you should mention it." Emi slid her phone across the table. Fae's mouth dropped as she read his message.

"Shit, Em. When did he send this to you?"

"On the way to brunch. Right after I thought someone said my name."

Fae feigned falling out of her chair.

"Well, you're going then."

"I . . . no. No, I can't do that. That would be crazy." Emi emphatically shook her head. "That would be just wrong. Like, I would blow up my whole life."

"Okay," Fae said patiently. "Tell me why. Why would it be wrong? Are you going to sleep with him?"

"Absolutely not. No."

"Are you going to leave Josh?" Again, Emi said no. "Would you even lie about where you were going?"

"No, I would tell Josh I was meeting an old friend. Of course, I would have to omit all this other shit. I couldn't tell him what I've been feeling. It would crush him."

Fae began counting on her fingers. "So, you wouldn't lie, cheat, or leave and ruin your family. I'm a Jesse-hater as much as the next best friend, but Em, I don't see what the problem is."

"I'm just scared, okay? I'm afraid that I might still have feelings for him," Emi said, hanging her head. "And worse, he doesn't for me. But I'm mostly afraid I'll find that maybe I'm unhappy. Or that I'll feel like I'm not where I should be. Do you think I'm unhappy?"

Fae took Emi's hand in hers and looked her in the eye. "Em, I know you better than anyone. Maybe even Josh. Oh, please don't cry."

Emi stuck her fingers in the corners of her eyes, trying to absorb the tears before they dropped.

"This doesn't mean you're unhappy."

"I'm just a terrible person," Emi lamented. "What kind of a wife or mother am I?"

"A great one. You're a person, Emi, with people feelings that are almost never black and white. Being a human is messy, and all you can do is your best. Trust me, I know."

"I keep trying to forget about Jesse and focus on my life. But then, five minutes later, some coincidence smacks me across the face and brings me back again. He likes one of my posts, or I see someone who looks exactly like him, and I spiral."

"I get it. I can't believe I'm saying this, but I think you should go. You'll see him, and yeah, I'm sure you still have feelings. He's clearly your twin flame. But I also think you will leave knowing you are exactly where you're meant to be, regardless of whether Jesse is your soulmate or if you have some other cosmic attachment binding you two together," Fae said. "You know what we need to do? We need to see my psychic."

"Your psychic?" Emi balked.

"If anyone can tell us what the fuck is going on, it's her."

CHAPTER NINE

A short woman with teased blond hair poked her head around the corner and beckoned ethereally for Emi to follow. She shot Fae a glance of trepidation, followed the woman to her office, and took a seat on a deep blue velvet couch next to a large curio cabinet filled with sparkly gemstones.

"Nice to meet you, Emi. I am Shannon. I'm a psychic and medium. I communicate with the other side through tarot readings and visions."

She paused and looked at Emi, who was nervously clutching her bag on her lap, with soft eyes. "Have you had readings before?" Shannon asked.

"Yes, I have. But not for a long time."

"Is there something specific that you came to me for?"

"Yes."

Shannon picked up a candle and rubbed oil around the base before lighting it.

"I would like us to both close our eyes in silence so that I can tune in and ask Spirit to come forward and help me see. Please take a deep breath, try to relax, and then concentrate on your question for me."

Emi tried to do as she was told. But her heart was hammering, and stray thoughts pulled her in every direction at once. She hoped Shannon would be able to see into the swirling monsoon of her mind.

"Someone has come back into your life," she stated after a pause. Emi caught her breath. "Nothing has happened in this dimension. At least, not yet. But you're feeling his energy very strongly, and it's throwing yours out of balance."

"Well, I am having dreams about somebody, and I feel like a lot of other strange things have been happening to me, too. Like, weird coincidences. And I think maybe they mean something, but I'm not sure what."

"I'm seeing a bluebird," Shannon said, opening her eyes. "She is your spirit guide, and she comes to you to help keep you on track. She says she's come to you with messages, but you aren't listening. The Universe continues to try to reach you, but you're writing it all off as imagination."

Emi remembered the little surprise visitor after her run around the river a few months earlier.

"Yes," she said, her brain churning. "I did see a bluebird a bit ago. And, if I think about it, maybe I've seen them for a while. That's my spirit guide?"

"Yes, dear. And I'm sure she's been around your whole life. You have more power and intuition than most, honey. Fear of truth cannot keep it at bay, and denying it will lead to anxiety and depression. Stop pretending that the signs from the Universe aren't serendipitous, even if they aren't giving you the answer you want. You know better than that. Why ask for help if you're not willing to acknowledge it? Now, when did these 'strange things' begin?"

"They started the morning of my birthday."

"And how old are you now?"

"Forty." Shannon smiled and nodded to herself as if she had a secret. "The dreams came first. Super vivid dreams, like you said. Almost as if they were real."

"Just because they're dreams doesn't mean they aren't real. In some cases, they may be more so than life. Your dream state is another dimension where we can meet with our guides and loved ones, past or present. And the two of you are together when you're dreaming about him. But go on."

That idea seemed too far-fetched for Emi's brain to comprehend, so she let it slide over her and continued.

"And I started seeing the same numbers and letters that coincide with this person somehow. I'm also hearing his name over and over, like, everywhere. Sometimes I even think I see him." Emi flushed. "And the more

I see or hear these things, the more they keep coming. They're jumping out at me when I'm driving, on TV, or at any other random place. They're everywhere I look."

"Oh, dear," Shannon tutted, noticing her worry. "Coincidences don't exist, sweetheart. They're just something we made up to explain away things that we don't understand or want to acknowledge, usually because they make us uncomfortable. These synchronicities are breadcrumbs from the spirit world. They're telling you something important. Do not ignore them. There's always a reason," she said. "This man's name—does it begin with a J?"

"Um, yes. It's Jesse."

"Jesse is trying to get in touch with you subconsciously. And many of these things you notice around you are him trying to reach you. He may not even be aware of what he is doing."

"I'm not sure what you mean. How could he get in touch with me subconsciously?"

"Through his energy. Think of the energy between people as cell phone waves, connecting you to everyone else in the world. Our subconsciouses can reach out through energetic frequencies, each acting like a phone number. Your energy frequency is a direct line to you, and my frequency is a direct line to me, each unique only to that person. We think time and physical space separate us in all ways, but they only do so physically. We are reachable through so much more, anywhere in the universe and at any point in history.

If someone is thinking about you a lot, it's as if they're texting you, wherever you are. These messages arrive through many means, like hearing someone's name repeatedly or seeing their initials or their birthday. They surface in dreams, songs, animals, and other repetitive ways. We also receive guidance from angels, loved ones, and our guides in these ways. Most people, however, aren't aware enough to even notice what's going on around them."

"Are these synchronicities happening to Jesse, too?"

"Absolutely. That's how it works. Jesse thinks about you, and then you get pinged to think of him. Then he gets pinged back from your thoughts and thinks about you again. It's like a game of continuous phone tag. But I see he's just as confused about it as you are. It's one of our many human disabilities." She sighed. "We have forgotten how powerful and connected we are. But you, Emi, are beginning to wake up. You are a seer and always have been. And this is all part of stepping into your power."

"My power?"

"Yes. You have the Eye, the Gift. And you already know the answers to what you have come to me for. But you don't want to listen to yourself because you fear what it might mean. So, you're looking for me to tell you something that won't challenge your life the way it is. But everything that happens has a purpose and a meaning. And many times, it's not what we want, but what we need."

Shannon let a few moments of silence between them linger while she allowed her words to percolate.

"You are married, but Jesse is not your husband." Emi nodded. "Even still, he is feeling like things are unfinished between you two. Is that correct?"

"Maybe. But it can't be unfinished because nothing ever began. It was cut short, whatever it was."

"What you two had was fated to be stifled, as if somebody abruptly blew out the flame. But you are still tied just as tightly to each other. Your connection runs deep in the spirit world, so you feel it now, too."

"What exactly is the spirit world?"

"It is what we call everything that is not of this dimension. There is so much more than our tiny speck of a planet, even if we cannot see it." She gently cleared her throat. "Emi, I'd like you to try something. Please uncross your legs, sit up straight, and close your eyes."

Emi did as she was told. Her mind went dark as her nostrils sucked in the thick air infused with lavender, but Emi thought she detected the faintest hint of evergreen. Her lungs expanded and contracted, lifting and sinking in a deep rhythm.

"Now, this time, I want you to clear your mind of all thought. Picture Jesse's face. Feel him next to you. Focus on your breath in, then out. You will hear my crystal bowl sing, but try to feel, not think."

Shannon played the crystal bowl, and the purest of sounds reverberated through Emi's whole body like ripples of water. In her mind's eye, she saw herself sitting on the sofa and looked on as a beam of white light broke through the ceiling and shone directly into the crown of her head. It filled her body from the top all the way down to her feet.

A man stood before her, his dark, almond eyes smiling. His pitch-black hair shimmered almost blue in the hot sun. The edges of his linen tunic flapped in the wind, and a wooden Coptic cross sat heavily on his chest.

He took her bronze hand in his, and a smile crept across her face to match. She pulled up her scratchy sheath dress in the other so as not to get dusty on the red road as they strode in their worn leather sandals toward the marketplace.

A little boy with skin the color of roasted chestnuts laughed as he skipped around them, swinging an empty clay pitcher, ready to be filled. She was happy.

Emi opened her eyes.

"What did you see, my dear?" Shannon asked.

"That was crazy," Emi breathed, shocked at her vision. "I saw him. It was Jesse, though it didn't look like him. He was much darker and shorter but had the same eyes." Shannon nodded for her to go on. "He held out his hand to me, and we were just walking. We had a son, he was beautiful."

"Did you get any sense of where or what time period?"

Emi remembered the dusty, red terrain and their simple clothes. "The desert somewhere. The Middle East, maybe Egypt. And he had on this necklace that looked like it was from a long time ago, maybe antiquity or before."

"Let's try it again," Shannon said.

Emi closed her eyes, and Shannon played the bowl, its frequency and sound melting together like butter. All she could feel was the slow and steady beat of her heart.

Her little, dimpled hand was wrapped tightly around her father's thick pinky. The wind and salt water whipped so fast, chilling her to the bone, that she could barely feel her fingers anymore. Her brown curls catching on her crackling lips, she wiped her hair away from her pudgy face and looked up at him with reverence.

He bent over and scooped her up, and she wrapped her arms around him and laid her head in the curve of his dirty neck.

"We're almost there, cailín leanbh. Almost there."

Suddenly, shouts began to spread across the deck of the enormous steamship like a wave. The third-class deck was so crammed full of people that she couldn't even see the floor on which they stood. Cheers broke out all around them, along with old Celtic folk songs and hats waved high.

"Da, why are you crying?" she asked, brow furrowed with concern.

"I'm crying because I'm happy, leanbh. We've made it all this way. Look!"

Her father pointed off into the distance. In a haze of fog, layered on top of the gray still water from which it rose, an enormous statue loomed. She wondered at the vast, green lady and her blazing torch, the likes she had only heard of in fairy tales, afraid of what came next.

But her fears subsided as her eyes fell on a young boy in a tattered coat. He sat proudly on a pair of shoulders, surrounded by a sea of jovial Irishmen. The sun poked out of the silvery mist, just for a moment, and lit up his red hair, which shone like copper in the light.

As if she had called him by name, the boy turned directly to her, his dark brown eyes dancing, and smiled.

Emi jolted awake. Shannon's face had replaced the little boy's, and she watched her expectantly, inviting her to speak.

"What did you see?"

"I saw the Statue of Liberty. I was a little girl, maybe five or six. We were immigrants."

Shannon nodded. "Was anyone else with you?"

"My father," Emi said. "And Jesse. He was a little boy this time. I know it was him."

"Good, good," Shannon said. Emi sat, mouth slacked, gaping at what she just experienced.

Even when I was an acid-tripping teenager, I never hallucinated like that.

Shannon got up again and retrieved a box of tarot cards from her cabinet. As she sat down, she handed them to Emi to shuffle and then asked for them back. She murmured to herself as she flipped over eight cards on the table for Emi to see.

"You found him," Shannon said.

"Jesse?"

"Yes, you found him in time. You two have spent thousands of lives together, and what you saw was just a sample. I was right about your connection. Together, you are a set of Primaries, the strongest romantic soul connection one can have." She tapped on the first card. "Like I said, the two of you have spent most of your lives destined to be together in some way or another. But your last life left you very sad. See here?"

She pointed at another card.

"This represents your previous life, which could be your last vision—the one with your father coming to America. This card here is the Empress, you on your wedding day." Shannon closed her eyes. "You were breathtaking in a cream-colored gown with buttons down the back. The two of you were happy. Until something he did, or maybe didn't do, and he ruined everything. But your problems weren't of fidelity or romance. You were both completely committed and dedicated to each other, you especially. Sometimes love isn't enough.

He left you to raise the children by yourself. He may even have committed suicide, and you never recovered. Whatever happened wasn't in the plan. Now, he is the one who needs to learn from that pain and is living out his negative karma in this lifetime.

Am I right that he's not married and has no kids?" Emi nodded. "He's had romantic love and will again, but it will only be surface and fleeting. Jesse's soul took for granted what he had with you, and living a life without you and your children now is the consequence."

Shannon paused as Emi sat wide-eyed and speechless on the sofa.

"And you now have the stability and happiness with your husband and family you wanted so badly with Jesse. You are living out your positive karma. Nothing is perfect, and there will be good times and bad, but when I see your life now, I am shown a full-circle rainbow, which I rarely see. You've earned this happiness, so enjoy it. Rest easy that you are exactly where you are supposed to be." Shannon patted Emi's hand kindly.

"Why is all of this happening now? Okay, we are soulmates, or whatever, and we are supposed to live separate lives. I get that. But what's the deal with the timing of all of this?"

"Something happens when we turn forty years old. We are about halfway through our life cycle. Instead of our lives being all about research, from birth until now, they turn to a time of analysis. We begin to reflect on our experiences and what we have learned so far. Only after we look back and process it all can we move forward into our soul's purpose.

If you have been pushing off certain things, refusing to experience them in the past, and running away from them, you will experience them much more intensely now. And those lessons keep coming back, usually in different forms, until we've truly dealt with them. The longer we procrastinate learning, the harder it becomes.

This is all happening now because Jesse is reflecting on his life and finally facing his regrets. You just happen to be a big one, both in this life and the last."

"So, then," Emi wondered aloud. "Is all this just for him to figure out, or is there something I'm supposed to learn, too?"

"Nothing is ever one-sided. You have multiple lessons to learn, but I can only share one, or it would be cheating." Shannon winked at her, flipped the top card of the tarot deck, and laid it on top of the others.

"All these experiences you're having—the synchronicities and dreams—are waking you up. The Universe is a living thing, and it's smart. It knows your Primary bond with Jesse was lingering in your subconscious, and it's strong enough to kick you in the head and get you to pay attention."

"Pay attention to what?"

"The spiritual, Emi. That's why you ended up on my couch. The fact that you could tap into your gift with very little guidance from me shows me not just how powerfully connected you are, but that you're ready to take the next step. Take control and hone your abilities."

"Are you saying I'm psychic, like you?"

"Yes, but in your own way."

"So, my dreams are actually prophetic? Rosie's going to love that," Emi mused.

"They are. Visions come to you, and you know things. But you've spent your whole life closing your intuitive door. Now is the time to open it.

When you're ready, I want you to go to this store and buy this book. Once you've read it, come back to me." She jotted the title on the back of a business card and handed it to Emi.

CHAPTER TEN

Jesse

The scar above Jenna's nose from her Big Wheel accident when she was four years old always ran red when she was angry. Usually, Jesse found it amusing, but today, it made him nervous.

"Oh, my God, Jesse. When is this supposed to happen?" Jenna asked skeptically as she carried a full laundry basket of clean clothes into her modest living room.

"Tomorrow, sometime. She told me to message her."

"I don't see how you could even contemplate meeting up with this girl," she said.

"Why? It's not like I'm planning on sleeping with her." Jesse diverted his gaze out of the window, unable to meet her hawkish glare.

"That doesn't mean you don't want to," she sneered under her breath. Jesse shot her a look.

"It's not like that. We're just friends."

"Do you have feelings for her?"

"Like what?"

"You know exactly what I mean." Jenna rolled her eyes. "This is the same girl who you've casually mentioned on and off for decades. I get that you think I haven't noticed that self-suffering little whisp in your voice when you find any excuse to mention her and then cryptically change the subject, but I know you, Jess. Plus, she's gorgeous. So, whatever you say, just cut the crap and tell me the truth."

Jesse was taken aback. "Okay, sis. Do you notice everything?"

"Yes," Jenna said. "I'm a girl."

"I mean, okay, yeah, she is beautiful," he confided with a shrug. "I just don't see what that has to do with anything."

"It has everything to do with everything. Jesse, you're my older brother, and I love you. And nobody else will say it, so I'm going to tell you that you're being a fucking idiot."

"I haven't told anyone else. And honestly, Jenna, don't you think you're being a little harsh?" He didn't know what else to say. He hated it when she put him on the spot like this. Mostly because she was almost always right.

"I've watched you sacrifice so much of your happiness for almost our whole lives."

"Jen, please—"

"No, let me say this. When Dad left, you became my father. You were our protector, the one who held the three of us together. You cooked dinner and checked if I did my homework. Mom was a wreck, but you were always steady and made sure we were both okay. You looked out for us then and now for Caleb, too.

If it weren't for you, I may not have even had him."

"Come on now, that's just not true," Jesse interjected.

"It is true. The thought of being a single mom seemed impossible, but you've been with me every step of the way. Who knows what you had to sacrifice for us along the way."

Jesse was never comfortable with this amount of honesty.

Why does Jenna always have to be so damn dramatic?

"You were the one who was in the hospital room and held my hand when I was in labor. You got up with me in the middle of the night when Caleb was a newborn and paid the bill when he had pneumonia. You taught him to ride a bike and throw a baseball. You've been here for every first day of school. There's a reason that you're the one that celebrates Father's Day with us and not his dad, who's off God knows where."

"But, Jen, that's my job. We're family. You are there for me, too. We look out for each other. And anyway, what does any of this have to do with Emi?"

"If you stop interrupting me, I'll fucking tell you. I think it's clear we've been a burden on you," Jenna said sadly. "We've been holding you back. I think maybe if you had less of us, you might have more room for someone else."

"How could you say that? You've never been a burden."

"I've watched you run from every relationship when it came time to commit. You've been jumping from girl to girl, never giving anyone a chance, and purposefully finding the youngest, dumbest ones in the room. I get it. Dad fucked you up. He fucked us all up. But that doesn't mean you need to take my shit on, also."

"I'm happy the way things are," Jesse said, though he wasn't sure that was completely accurate. "Plus, it's always just been you, me, Mom, and Caleb. You guys need me."

"That's nothing but a cop-out, Jesse, and you know it. I know you want to find someone and start a family of your own. And I also know you look at Emi's pictures online with her kids and her Christmas-card life when you think no one's around.

Don't look at me like that. She's all over your search history."

"Jesus Christ, Jenna, are you going through my phone?"

"That's not the point. I also see the relationship you have with Caleb, and I know what an amazing father you would be. If anyone deserves it, it's you. All we want for you is to fall in love with someone great and live happily ever after."

Oh my God, can this conversation be over yet?

Jenna stopped furiously folding the laundry, picked up his phone from the coffee table, and tapped Emi's profile picture on the screen.

"My point is, this girl can't give any of that to you."

Jesse felt his throat close. For the first time in a long time, he thought he might cry. "Yeah, but—"

"She can't give it to you because she already has it. Nothing will change the fact that she's fucking married and she is very happy."

Jesse winced. Like an arrow through the heart, it hurt him to know how happy Emi was in her life, and it was even worse to hear it from someone else.

"You said her son is close to Caleb's age, and she's got two other kids? You want to crush their lives, too?"

"Enough with the crucifixion already. You know I'd never hurt Emi's or anyone else's kids. Ever."

"Remember how devastated we were when Dad left, and how angry you were when Rob walked out on me when I was pregnant? And now, you're going to do that to another family?"

"I said enough!" Jesse boomed, more forcefully than he meant. "Fuck."

Silence fell between them, and Jesse knew he had hurt her feelings.

"I'm just saying," Jenna said after a while. "If you meet her tomorrow, you're just going to get your heart broken."

Jesse sighed and let her finish. Jenna reached out and laid a soft hand on his.

"And even if we surmise that she does feel the same way, nothing will come of it except hurt. And not just for you, but for her, too.

Jesse, I'm afraid that if this goes poorly, you will never stick your little turtle head out of your soft shell ever again."

All the dreams that felt so real, all the times he thought about her over the years, or saw her smile on some faceless stranger—did none of it ever matter?

I need to know. I need to look Emi in the face and see for myself if anything is there. I'm not going to hurt anyone. Jenna just doesn't get it.

"You're still going to go, aren't you?"

"I have to, Jenna. I can't tell you why. I just feel it," he implored. She shook her head.

"Uncle Jesse!" Caleb came bounding through the doorway, a toothless grin wrapped around his face, bringing his own sunshine to lighten the room. He flung his backpack to the floor and jumped on Jesse's thick back, pouncing like a tiger cub. Jesse stood up to let him dangle, then tickled his armpits until he fell off in hysterics.

"Hey, kiddo. Told you I'd come," Jesse said. He allowed his nephew to get him in a headlock, then easily plucked him from the floor and tossed him on the couch.

"Alright, alright," Jesse heaved, "go easy on me, kid."

"You're out of shape, old man."

"Okay, you two." Jenna threw a clean shirt from the folded pile at her son. "Caleb, honey, change and get washed up for dinner. Your uncle's taking us out."

Caleb's large eyes looked to Jesse, who nodded behind Jenna's back, telling him to go.

"That little boy loves you so much," Jenna said, wagging a stern finger in his face. "He looks up to you, Jesse, so be careful here. The decision you make tomorrow could end up ruining not just your life, but so many others."

Jesse's insides shrunk and shriveled, collapsing in on himself. Just the idea broke something in him.

He could never hurt his nephew. He loved that little boy more than anything.

"Jesse?" Emi called with the playfulness of hide-and-seek. "There you are!"

She rounded the bend in the trees, and her brilliant smile, illuminated in the blue-purple light of the darkened sky, melted his heart. After all this time, just the sight of her still had him flustered like a lovesick teenager.

The still winter night surrounded them, the woods quiet as could be. Snow-covered pines towered into the dark sky and brushed the stars that twinkled in her eyes.

She was never more radiant.

"Jesse, what's wrong?"

"How do you know something's wrong?"

"I can feel it," she said, saddening with each crunchy step that brought her closer.

Plump snowflakes wafted around her in the thin air, sparkling like stardust in her golden glow. Emi pulled herself into her puffy coat, and Jesse marveled at how cute she was when her nose turned red from the cold. She reached up and put a gloved hand on his cheek.

It wasn't fair when she looked at him like that. How could he say what he needed to say with those brown eyes, so unconditional and loving, peering expectantly into his own?

"Tell me, please."

"I can't come," he choked out. "I can't meet you tomorrow."

Her face fell, and the worst happened. Betrayal flashed across it. She took a step back, so he took one forward.

"I want to. You know how much I want to."

Her despair shattered his heart into a million tiny pieces. "I love you. More than anything, more than the sun, and the moon, and the stars. For all eternity, literally. Please don't be mad."

Emi turned away, but he pulled her close.

"Come here, you're shivering," he said.

"No. I'm not angry, Jesse. I'm just so disheartened. I thought you were ready. You told me you were ready." She huffed as she broke his embrace.

Her words sunk him like a ship.

"But you know I can't come. I can't compromise us like that, Em. We have to pass this test. We have to do it right and get back to each other."

"Life isn't a test, Jesse. It's not pass-fail." She sighed in resignation. "You promised after last time that you'd come for me, that you'd fix it."

He dropped his head. "Emi, these are the paths we've chosen. You're right, life isn't a test. But it is a karmic reward system, and if we go tomorrow, it will only make it worse."

"No, you will make it better by telling me how you feel, even if you get nothing in return. Don't you understand? It's the courage to stand in your feelings that you have to find. What happens between us after tomorrow isn't the point. It's the showing up that counts. You ran away in our last life.

I've been waiting for you to choose me over fear for a century now. I won't wait much longer. You have to be brave for us, Jesse, please," she begged.

She's right. I let us both down before, and now I'm afraid I will again.

"I'm not as strong as you, Emi. I never have been. You've always been the one leading the way. I'm lost without you."

"Well, it's time for you to step up and find your own compass." Fat tears sparkled like icicles as they rolled down her face. "I will be there. I hope you will, too," she said with the stabbing coolness of finality.

An owl hooted in the distance, and Jesse turned his head. But before he turned back, he knew she was gone. He stood alone in the snowy woods, the heat from his breath catching in the moonlight, and cried.

Jesse asked the Uber driver to pull over a block away. Jenna's warning still circled in his head as he climbed out of the car and made his way through the busy city toward his destination.

Now that Emi was only minutes away, everything in his body and soul wanted him to sprint toward the diner where she sat, stopping for nothing until he saw her again. It was a biological pull, like the waves to the moon. But the closer he got the louder his sister's words and his anxiety became.

The cars honking in the busy intersection barely registered. Pedestrians passed him on the sidewalk, a biker zipped in and out, and a pair of yappy dogs on leashes barked at each other from across the street, but he paid no mind to any of it. The world around slipped into a blur of white noise until he looked up and found himself standing across the street from a large fifties-inspired neon sign that read *Pamela's*.

He was there. Jesse checked his watch. He was a couple of minutes late, probably from his tortured debate about which T-shirt to wear, though it seemed superfluous now.

The crosswalk sign blinked on, and he began to cross. His heart pounded, and each step brought a new and terrifying worry.

What if Emi stands me up? What if she decides I'm old and unattractive? What if we have nothing in common, or she thinks I'm boring?

Most ominous though, was his circular obsession with the idea he really might want more from her than a platonic lunch. And even worse, if the feeling was mutual.

He swallowed hard. By the time he reached the curb in front of the diner, Jesse was so dizzy, he almost had to sit down on its stoop. Jenna was right. No good would come of their meeting.

What the hell am I doing?

But before he could stop himself, he caught a glimpse of someone through the window.

It was her. She sat alone in a red booth, with her back to him, chocolate hair shining in the sunlight, long and soft. He had a vision of running his fingers through it.

His soul felt the warm and tender tug toward that booth, like the streetlamps at dusk, ushering him back to his childhood home. But he shoved it aside and followed his mind somewhere else.

If you really care about her, you'll stay away.

As he looked at Emi through the glass, he suddenly and finally understood the weight of his feelings and the damage they could do. Then words came to him that made no sense.

"It's not the right time, Em," he whispered as he put his hand up to the glass. "Not yet."

The debate was over. After months of torment, he had finally made up his mind. Jesse turned on the spot and forced himself not to look back.

CHAPTER ELEVEN

Jesse could barely bring himself to grunt at Jenna when she'd asked about the diner from the doorway of her guest bedroom. He felt his sister's concern emanating from the hallway. After lingering for a minute or two, she shut his door and left him to sprawl on the bed and bury his head under his pillow like an angsty preteen.

Sleep eluded him. He tossed and turned with the thought of Emi, waiting for someone who would never come.

She definitely hates me now.

Jesse's ego played cruel propaganda reels in his mind, and he cringed as his imagination got the better of him.

Maybe Emi had gone home to laugh with her handsome husband about the boy below her station she'd rejected so many years ago. She would have told him how he'd obsessed over her for decades and somehow got up the false courage to ask her to lunch, only to run away, weak and fearful.

"I bet he's still in love with you," he heard Josh say smugly, like a kid with the biggest piece of cake.

"Ew, never," Emi snickered. "I didn't like him then, and certainly not now. No self-respecting woman would ever pick Jesse Amato."

In his mind's eye, he saw her gossiping with her girlfriends at the playground. They sat around in a circle while their perfect little kids played on the jungle gym and called him a stalker, hypothesizing about why he was still single. They would diagnose him with Peter Pan Syndrome and all agree that she was better off.

These scenes wrenched his gut and engorged his embarrassment. But an even worse picture came to him.

Maybe Emi sat in that large red booth, her brown eyes hopeful and excited, watching every person who walked past. With each minute that ticked by, she shrank smaller and smaller. She checked her phone and reread his final message.

Can't wait!

Emi left the diner heartbroken and angry, vowing never to speak to him again.

How could he have just left? God, he was such an idiot.

Jesse couldn't help but constantly refresh his social media, willing a little red notification to appear in the top right corner of his screen. He typed out a multitude of excuses for why he didn't show up: His nephew was sick, his dog ran away, he had car trouble. But none of them made sense, and Emi was smarter than that anyway.

When sleep finally found him, it was fitful and anxious, with dreams of a violent storm ripping up a forest and expelling all the birds who lived there. But he picked himself up the next morning with the rising sun and still managed to run five miles along the river and back.

As he rounded the corner to Jenna's modest street and climbed the steps to her little brick house, he made up his mind to let Emi go.

It was time. Twenty years of what-if had done nothing but torture him. He forced a smile for Caleb's sake and got on with his day.

Maybe he could convince himself Emi Klein was nothing more than a fever dream.

"Goodbye, buddy. Be good for your mom," Jesse said on the airport curb.

Only a few days had passed since he'd made the decision to splinter his own heart and pour Emi out of it. His grief was still fresh and piping hot, but he slid his melancholy frown under his hat and pulled his nephew in for a hug. Cars swooshed past Jenna's hatchback as they stood in front of the departure door, below planes shooting off in every direction.

"Bye, little sis," he said as he turned to Jenna, hugging her next. "I love you. Be good."

She looked at him with their mother's worried expression. "Jesse, it'll be okay. I know you're sad, but you did the right thing."

"Yeah, I know."

Depression spread through him, numbing his heart and body, making his limbs heavy as he put one foot in front of the other through the terminal. Saying goodbye to Caleb was always crushing. But leaving like this—as the asshole who stood up the maybe love of his life—felt like someone tied an anchor to his ankle and tossed him into the river.

As he waited for boarding to begin, his head went round and round like luggage on the tram. Jesse's phone buzzed, and his hopeful heart burst; it was just a text from Jenna.

I'm worried. You okay?

What could he say? She knew him well enough to catch his lies, even over text. Jesse silenced his phone.

He boarded the plane and smiled at the flight attendant. He shut his leather carry-on in the compartment above his first-class seat and helped a woman behind him struggling with her bag. Cool and collected, even thoughtful and polite on the outside, Jesse's mind was still reeling inside.

In Colorado, he was Jesse Amato, a completely self-made, desirable man who pulled in seven figures a year. Jesse didn't strive to portray the Instagram life; he lived it.

He had a beautiful home in Aspen and a lengthy investment portfolio. He took his family and friends on lavish vacations, and he'd reached his goal of setting foot on every continent two times over. Jesse was a boss, not some insecure teenager who second-guessed every move he made.

Yes, it was time to go home and remember who the fuck he was.

The plane backed away from the terminal and taxied around the runway. It picked up speed, and the rush of the engine gunning ran through Jesse's stomach as the wheels lifted off the ground and pulled into the plane.

The city looked like a model train set, tiny cars puttering through doll-sized neighborhoods. He wondered if one of them was Josh Felice, heading home after a long day at the office, to Emi and their kids for dinner, foolishly unaware of how lucky he was.

She'd be in the kitchen cooking chicken cutlets and helping Jack with his math homework. Her husband would walk through the door to hugs and kisses and tell them about his day, and she would say how proud she was of him. They'd clean up and laugh together with a glass of wine in front of the fire. Maybe they'd even read to their little one, tuck him in safely, and then retreat to their bedroom, where he would get her all to himself. Forever.

The plane flew into a blanket of mist, and when it emerged on top, a vast, puffy ocean of clouds swallowed the city below. He watched the sun set pink and orange on the horizon.

Night tiptoed over the sky and they soared through the darkness, the jet engine plane humming serenely. Jesse opened his laptop to get some work done but couldn't concentrate. Depleted, he leaned his seat back and shut his eyes, willing his brain to empty for the long trip ahead.

A pocked moon hung in the sky, and the forest was still and dark. The treetops stood solemnly at attention, cloaked in shadow. The wildflowers were stiff, and not a living thing stirred in the quiet, abandoned meadow.

Emi

How could I be so dumb? I knew he wouldn't show up, somehow. But I sat in that diner anyway, like an idiot moth to an avoidable flame. God, I'm stupid.

Emi put the wet clothes in the dryer, slammed the door, and walked back to her bedroom to glue Liam's newly awarded patches onto his Boy Scout vest. Maddie followed her every step, tail wagging, and jumped up on the bed next to her. She kept so close Emi thought maybe she could feel her despondency. The dog had been extra needy lately, staying only inches away from Emi since the day she got home from the diner.

She had come that day into the house with an Oscar-winning smile only a mom could fake. Emi put her purse down and started dinner right away. She was extra cheery that night, laughing over her lasagna with Jack and reading Liam three books instead of his usual two at bedtime. She bought Vi the pricy skincare she'd been begging for and stayed up late to watch one of Josh's favorite slasher movies with him, which she hated. She made love with renewed affection and appreciation for her husband, who only ever wanted to make her happy, followed through with his promises, and treated her like the queen he always told her she was.

But after a while, Emi found herself in quiet moments sorrowful, and not indifferent like she would have hoped. Now, as she sat on the bed, she stared blankly out of her bedroom window, glue stick in hand, numb.

"Mom?" Violet asked from the open doorway. "You look sad. Are you okay?"

Emi wondered how long she had been standing there, watching her mother sit cross-legged on the bed, withdrawn inside herself. When Josh asked about her lunch, she had given him a short, unaffected "something came up" and waved it off. But she hadn't been able to hide as effectively from her daughter. Violet knew her best, was sensitive to Emi's idiosyncrasies, and seemed to pick up on her unspoken melancholy.

"Oh, uh, hi honey." Emi flashed a fake smile as she quickly moved her phone off her lap. "Yes, I'm fine. I'm just thinking, is all."

Violet looked at her skeptically, big-eyed and worried, like a little girl.

"Well, I'm going to Sydney's. Unless you want me to stay? We could watch *Gossip Girl*."

"I would love that. But you go have fun with Syd. We can watch it tomorrow."

Violet walked over to Emi and draped her in a hug. "I love you, Mamma."

"Love you too, sweets."

The organic grocery store buzzed with people in hemp beanies or designer clothes as they picked out their ethically sourced, non-GMO produce, grass-fed and pasture-raised meats, and smelly, artisan cheeses. Emi dawdled behind as she stuck her nose in each of the fresh bouquets of flowers, admiring their sweetness as she breathed them in.

"You still haven't heard anything?" Fae asked bitterly, reaching for a carton of almond milk.

Emi shook her head, moving her attention to the grocery list on her phone. A week now had passed since the lunch rendezvous that wasn't, and she'd already purged Jesse from her social media accounts without a word.

"Like, nothing?"

"Like, nothing. But I don't know what you expect him to do now. I gave it twenty-four hours before I pulled the plug." Emi shrugged. She stood on her tiptoes to grab a bag of organic chips from the top of the aisle.

"I thought he would message you with some lame excuse at least. Ghosting you is even less than I expected from him. Which frankly says a lot."

Emi kept walking. What could she say? At least it was over. No more wondering what might have happened between them so long ago.

"Well, that kid doesn't deserve to see your life anyway. What an asshole," Fae said, shaking her head. "Please tell me you finally hate him as much as I do now."

"Yes," Emi lied.

No, I don't hate him. But I do feel really stupid. All I wanted was to look him in the face and find out for myself if there really was anything there.

"Honestly, I'm just embarrassed about the whole thing. I can't believe I let some dude I don't know live rent-free in my mind for so long, especially when I have such an amazing life. And he couldn't even give me the time of day."

Emi couldn't say the rest out loud—that she'd allowed herself to be pulled to that diner by some invisible force haunting her dreams, just waiting to paint her a fool.

"Jesse's the one who should be embarrassed. No wonder he's single." Fae handed Emi the salsa she was looking for. "Jesse's just another man-child. Probably stuck in his college glory days, terrified to grow up, and bringing down all the women around him."

"I know this sounds super weird. But I think I just liked having a secret, all to myself. Like, I've given every part of myself away to Josh and the kids, and it felt good to have something innocuous just for me. Even if it was just a silly little crush."

"That's not weird at all."

That's all this was. Just a bunch of complicated feelings, projected onto someone who didn't matter or affect my life in any way . . . right?

They turned the corner and made their way over to the bread. Emi was inspecting a crusty Italian loaf when her phone buzzed. A chill came over her. She pulled it out of her pocket and looked at the screen.

"What?" Fae asked when she saw her face.

"I just, I don't understand," Emi said. She handed the phone to Fae. The new-message notification was still on the screen, but her inbox was empty.

"This has happened a couple of times. At first, I thought it was a fluke or something."

"It's not a fluke, Em. Someone messaged you, but it was deleted right after."

"Who would do that?" Emi asked. Fae rolled her eyes.

"A coward."

Josh opened the car door, taking Emi's hand and delicately helping her in.

"We're going to the new Mexican place, right?" he asked once their seat belts were fastened.

"Yep. Reservation is at six, then the eight-thirty movie. I bought popcorn and drinks online. They'll bring it to our seats."

"Remember when you had to stand in line and wait your turn? When *Jurassic Park* came out, I stood on the street for over an hour and a half."

Emi smiled. "Remember when movie seats were those awful ridged, red things? You had to push the seat down, and it would pop up on you if you sat the wrong way? My purse always fell through the back."

"Oh my God, mine, too!" Josh teased. "And the floors were covered in gum and soda so your feet would stick to it like at a house party. Now there are heated leather recliners and lighted aisles. Man, I miss the nineties."

"Kids these days, they have no idea."

They drove for a bit, listening to music as Josh quietly sang along with his alternative station and drummed the steering wheel. The gray sky opened up into a drizzle, and Emi watched the water beads slide down her window.

"Do you think when you dream about someone, they're dreaming about you, too?"

She could tell her question caught him off guard. "What do you mean?"

"Like, if I'm dreaming about you, would you have your own dream about me? Or do you think our minds could meet up in our dreams?"

He flashed her an uncertain glance. "What are you thinking about in there?"

"I don't know, just wondering."

"I guess it's possible," Josh said.

Emi fell silent, lost in her head. At first, meeting with Shannon had provided relief that she and Josh were meant to be together in this life and that she was on the right course. But her thoughts eventually returned to their conversation about Jesse and the dreams they supposedly shared.

More unsettled than ever, Emi wished she could talk it all over with Josh, the person she was closest to. His personality was different from hers; he always had a tempered and pragmatic point of view, which usually helped. The feeling that she was keeping secrets from him made her skin crawl. She was jumpy and unnerved around him, like a sixteen-year-old who'd just smoked her first joint—paranoid, awkward, and desperate not to be found out.

But how could she explain all these existential questions that circled another man from a lifetime ago? He wouldn't understand.

"Do you think our lives are destined to be a certain way?" Emi asked, breaking the silence and her crushing guilt. "Like life is a map that's already plotted, and we are just following it?"

"Yes, I think some things are. I know we were," Josh said honestly, resting one hand on her thigh as he drove.

"Oh yeah?" Emi turned toward him with a soft, surprised smile.

"Sure. I couldn't tell you why I was at that ATM that night. The closest one to my apartment was on Ivy Street, not Walnut. And it was a last-minute decision for everyone to meet up in Shadyside anyway.

You know the story. We were supposed to leave for March Madness that afternoon, but the weather got bad, and we had to wait out the snow. But I had to stay after I ran into you on the street. I just knew if I walked away, I would regret it forever. I didn't care how annoyed the guys were. Something told me how important that moment was, and I wouldn't let you pass me by."

"Of course not, you wouldn't let me pass you by because you were hoping to get laid." Emi laughed.

"Em!" He chuckled. "No. It was my intuition. I bought you drinks the next weekend after I got home, hoping to get laid."

"So, what is your intuition telling you now?" Emi asked him with a cocked eyebrow and a crooked smile.

"To buy you drinks tonight, too."

"Aw, honey, save the money. I'm just as much fun sober."

But Emi's heart sank as Josh changed the station to eighties classics. "Jesse's Girl" struck up over the speakers, coming in hot. At the same time, a car pulled in front of them at a red light. She looked up, and her stomach dropped.

Its license plate read EJA-77. Emi almost screamed.

What else does the Universe want from me? When will these stupid signs stop? I just want it to be over!

Emi was doing what she thought she was supposed to. She had woken up to the synchronicities around her and was questioning life, just like Shannon instructed. Still, the stubborn signs of Jesse persisted. Waiting it out wasn't working.

When will Jesse Amato go away? Just leave me alone already!

That night, after a sweet evening away from the kids, she slipped into bed, kissed her husband, and pulled the comforter up to her chest. Emi closed her eyes tightly and prayed. She begged the Universe to let her dream good dreams, or anything, really, except Jesse Amato.

But when she woke the next morning, she knew her wish had not come true.

Jesse

Stella trotted up to Jesse through the patchy grass of the dog park. He gave her a quick back scratch before she was off again to run with the pack.

"You're so funny!" his date exclaimed, touching his shoulder and running her hand down his arm. It was a nice gesture, but he noticed the lack of spark he felt as her fingers grazed his skin.

Is it me, or is there just no chemistry? I can't tell anymore.

"Tell me about your tattoos?" he asked.

"Oh, well, this one is about my job," she said, pointing at a compass inked on her upper arm. Her blond hair blew in the summer breeze. "It says 'wanderlust' because I love traveling, which is why I'm a flight attendant. It's not my dream job, but I get a lot of travel perks. I'm hoping to get an international flight route at some point, maybe to Europe."

"That's awesome. When I was young, I had a dream of seeing every country. I'm not sure how feasible that is now because some places just aren't safe to visit. But I'm trying to get to each one that I can."

"I love that." She gave him a luring look and took a sip of the CBD-infused bubble tea he'd bought her on their walk.

"Are there any places you've wanted to go?" he asked.

"Oh, sure. I would love to get to Germany for Oktoberfest and see Big Ben. Oh, the Eiffel Tower and the Pointe des Arts Bridge. Have you heard of it?"

An invisible bullet struck him right through the chest.

"That's the one with the bicycle locks of love or whatever?" he stammered.

"Yeah, but it collapsed a while back because the locks were too heavy. I think people just take selfies on it now."

Huh. Seems fitting.

"Maybe when Paris is on your itinerary, we might see it together," she suggested coyly. Jesse's stomach pulled into itself.

"Sure," he said. He almost believed his own smile.

What the hell is wrong with me? This girl is great, why don't I feel anything?

In silence, they watched Stella chase a goldendoodle with a tennis ball in its mouth. Jesse tried to push away the memory of when he'd first learned about the Parisian bridge.

"Emmy!" a woman's voice called. "Emmy! Bring it back!"

Jesse looked up, frozen in terror.

"Emmy, come!" the woman demanded.

"That dog is so cute," his date said, watching the goldendoodle sprint the ball back to its owner. "She looks like a teddy bear."

"Yeah," Jesse said, repressing his frustration at the unwanted coincidence. "Cute."

God damn it. This girl is normal and nice, and we have things in common. She is pretty, and she likes me. It doesn't matter how many times a day Emi crosses my mind. I need to move on.

"I've gotta get going. Do you want to do drinks with me sometime?" he asked.

"I'd love to!"

"Emi?" Jesse called.

Only his anxious voice returned to him, echoing through the woods around their clearing. The trees danced sinisterly as storm clouds rolled through.

"Emi, I know you're still here. I can feel you." He almost jumped out of his skin as thunder clapped around him. "I fucked everything up. It's all my fault. It's always been all my fault. I'm so sorry, Emi, but I'm going to fix it. I swear."

CHAPTER TWELVE

2006
Emi

The bar was dark, smoky, and packed with people dressed head to toe in black and yellow. The mob of heads stared intently at the many TV screens and held their breath. It was Super Bowl Sunday in the Steel City, and snow fell quickly and silently outside.

The Steelers were playing the Seahawks, and Josh, Emi, Fae, and a large group of friends crowded into the tight bar, somehow snagging a table early on. Nobody was drunk yet because everyone wanted to have their wits about them for the game. The city collectively concentrated on sending all its energy toward the shiny gold trophy.

Saving their best play of the night for last, Coach Cowher's famous jaw clenched. You could hear a pin drop as Antwaan Randle El threw a forty-three-yard touchdown straight into Hines Ward's hands as he danced into the end zone like child's play. The bar patrons, clutching their Terrible Towels like rosaries, broke into a scream that seemed to rattle Earth to its core. The Steelers kicked the field goal and clinched the win.

Officially, the Pittsburgh Steelers won twenty-one to ten. Everyone was on their feet, jumping, yelling, whooping, beer spilling, and hugging, even the burliest of men with tears in their eyes. Glory and hometown pride were in the air as strangers became the best of friends for the night. Their yellow towels waved wildly, and Styx's "Renegade" boomed as the mass of people joined the chorus.

Amid the joyful chaos, Josh twirled Emi around as he sang along. He pulled her in tightly and whispered in her ear.

"I love you, Emelie Klein."

"I love you, too."

"Move with me to DC."

"Okay." Emi smiled. "On one condition."

"Anything."

"Wherever we go, I'll always be a Pittsburgh girl."

The sun had just begun to set on the Delaware shore, and the Atlantic Ocean sparkled orange and pink. Emi, Fae, and a half circle of friends sat in low beach chairs with their feet in the sand, watching the water and squawking seagulls. They indulged in old college stories, the latest work gossip, and the drama of young relationships, with beer cans and red plastic cups in hand.

The girls donned tiny bikinis and cut-off shorts, flaunting tanned, toned bodies. The boys wore swim trunks, cargo shorts, and backward baseball hats, showing off hard-earned muscles. A small speaker on a picnic blanket kicked out classic '80s rock, which had become cool again in its satirical nostalgia. Two large coolers filled to the brim with ice, beer, Jägermeister, Fireball, and a couple of bags of candy and chips lay on top in the center of the fun, waiting to be shared.

As the intro to the gang's favorite hair band song swelled, Josh and Greg dropped their football in the sand and made their way over. Josh picked Emi up from her chair and wrapped her legs around him as he stood. Their friends followed suit, singing and dancing in the sand, spinning each other around while the waves crashed beyond.

Later that evening, Emi showered and changed into her favorite white eyelet-embroidered crop top and denim miniskirt. She admired herself in the mirror, loving her dark hair streaked with golden highlights and her skin a deep bronze.

As she brushed her hair, she thought over the scene on the beach, and gratitude inflated her heart. Spending the week with her friends felt more special this year, though she wasn't sure why. Maybe it was because they were all growing up, floundering in the real world like little fish in a big, scary ocean. Maybe it was because living in a new city and making these friendships over the last year felt more meaningful than making friends in the safety of her campus grounds. Or maybe it was because she was with Josh, and everything felt more significant.

They had been living together for some time, and she was sure he wanted to be with her forever. That idea didn't scare Emi like it used to. Now, it just felt right.

She turned as Josh walked out of the closet. He had gone in there and shut the door, which made Emi quirk an eyebrow.

"Did you change your shirt again?" she teased. "That's, like, the third time in twenty minutes."

"I thought I saw a stain," Josh said, distracted.

"You look great." She smiled as she put the brush down and fixed the collar on his navy polo shirt. "We're just going for drinks anyway. It's not like it's a big deal. You've already got the girl, remember?"

Emi searched his face to meet his eyes. But before she could catch them, he turned on a dime and left the room. As quickly as he went, however, he came right back and gave her an abrupt hug and a kiss on the lips.

"I love you," Josh said seriously.

"I love you, too?" Emi stammered, then watched him walk out again.

He is acting so weird. Did I do something?

She followed his footsteps into the hallway, where she thought she heard whispering around the corner and bumped into Fae.

"Hey, have you seen my flip-flops?" Emi asked from behind. Fae almost jumped out of her skin.

"Oh! Emi, you scared me! No, sorry. They're probably in the living room. You look beautiful."

"Thanks. What the hell is happening? Josh is being super weird."

"Yeah, well, he's a twenty-six-year-old boy. They're all weird."

They joined the rest of their friends, gathering in the living room. Josh checked his cell phone, then made his way in front of the large fireplace and cleared his throat.

"Okay, before we head out, I have a surprise. If you could all kindly grab your drinks and meet me on the back porch."

Emi looked around the room. Nobody asked Josh what this was all about, not even Fae. The boys slapped him on the shoulder as they walked through the door, and the girls beamed with excitement.

Emi's nerves grabbed hold of her. She slowly put one foot in front of the other, heart pounding.

Oh my God. Is this it?

They all filed out onto the large wraparound porch of their rental house, coupled up, and peered out onto the darkened beach. The sky was almost entirely black, and the stars shone brighter by the second as the last hint of daylight succumbed to the night.

It was so quiet that she could hear the wind whistle and the waves crash in the distance. Josh and Emi were the last two out of the house, and she studied him as he took her hand and walked her to the bottom of the stairs, planting their feet in the sand.

Before she could ask any questions, something beyond the dune whizzed up into the air, cracked loudly, and boomed. Red, green, purple, and white fireworks lit up the sky.

Emi turned to Josh and found him down in the sand on one knee, waiting patiently and grinning at her.

"Emelie Colette, will you marry me?"

Roman candles burst above them and reflected in Josh's imploring eyes. His hands were trembling, and it occurred to her that she had never seen him nervous before. She sat on the leg he was leaning on and wrapped her arms around his shoulders, looking him square in the eye.

"Yes."

As if by a defense mechanism, protecting her from too much too quickly, Emi's mind slipped into a surreal state. She stood in the vestibule behind the large wooden synagogue doors, not unhappy but a little lost. Like a passive observer watching her busy bridesmaids flitting around in mismatched black dresses, readying bouquets of lilies, and finishing their flutes of champagne, she found herself in a lucid dream. Blinking, she tried to bring herself back from the snail's pace her brain was firing on, as everyone else seemed to be on fast-forward, excited for the moment to come.

Emi turned to the window, hoping the sunlight might wake her, and caught a glimpse of herself in the reflection. Her hair was up in a perfect chignon, and her ivory gown exposed her graceful neck and collarbone. But the fact that she was all done up and almost didn't recognize herself in her bridal glam only added to her dream-like state.

I really do look beautiful, though. Like a real bride.

Her mother fixed her father's bowtie in the corner as one last preparation. The string quartet began the procession music on the other side of the doors, and they opened dramatically. Two wedding planners buzzed around like bees, lining up five of Emi's closest girlfriends, plus Rose and Fae, straightening their gowns and fixing their lip gloss before disappearing further behind the scenes.

Emi waited pensively by the window, looking out into the summer sun, as they began their march down the aisle. Fae turned and smiled at her, but the look in her eyes said what Emi couldn't: something was off. She exchanged a quick, urgent glance with Rose in the last second before sweeping through the doorway and down the red carpet.

Her body was standing in the temple, dressed like a queen in her fitted gown and diamond headband, waiting patiently to be married. But her thoughts were lost somewhere far away and also deep within.

Rose had heard Fae's silent message loud and clear. She reached out and squeezed Emi's hand.

"Em. Emi. You ready? This is it," she whispered.

Emi jumped awake. Her sister's touch revived her and brought her back.

"Yeah, yes. Yes, I'm good. It's your turn, go!"

Rose gave her one more skeptical look, but Emi smiled reassuringly and shooed her through the doors.

She was left with only herself and the little bluebird that had just reappeared on the other side of the windowpane.

"Oh, I'm happy you came back," Emi said with a smile. "You almost missed it." When she arrived at the temple that morning, it sang sweetly on a branch above the doors and came to visit her in her bridal suite. Now, it took its seat on the stone sill to watch.

Emi's heart began to pound. It was her turn. She gripped her gorgeous bouquet, wrapped in a strand of her grandmother's pearls, and closed her eyes.

I will be happy. Josh will take care of me and love me faithfully and unconditionally; I love him so much, and marrying him is the right thing to do.

The heavy doors opened one last time, and with a final glance over her shoulder, Emi thought she saw the bird give her its blessing with a nod of encouragement. With that, she took a deep breath and stepped over the threshold.

Three hundred heads turned and gasped. Emi knew well what she looked like—her aesthetic carefully curated to be both angelic and expensive—as she floated down the aisle. The gown's open back teased her curves, and thousands of embroidered crystals sparkled in the dim temple lighting. The chuppah was covered top to bottom with white lilies and hydrangeas, and canopied Josh and her family's rabbi with ivory silk.

She had thought about this moment for months but didn't expect the excitement she would feel just looking at him. He was so handsome in his tux that her stomach flipped. They were locked in on each other, beaming like lovestruck teenagers.

Emi reached her almost-husband at the end of the aisle, and he took her hands in his. She turned to the window at the back of the sanctuary for one last look but found it empty. The little bird was gone.

The water was the brightest blue she had ever seen. The sun warmed Emi's brown skin as she walked down the bleached plaster steps that cascaded across the Santorini mountainside. A little sailboat bobbed up and down next to a weathered dock while a Greek sailor stood on the bow, smiling.

He called out to them. "Mr. and Mrs. Felice?"

"Are you going to tell me now?" Emi asked. Josh let loose an amused sigh.

"You are tenacious. Just get on the damn boat."

The sailor held out a hand to Emi. He hoisted her up, and Josh jumped in behind them.

"To Ammoudi, eh?" he asked Josh.

"Nai," Josh replied with a nod.

Emi's nervousness grew the closer they sailed to the large rock, and it soared as they waited in line at the top of the cliff for their turn. She focused on the beauty of the Mediterranean as it stretched out in front of them as far as they could see, blurring the horizon lines, but it didn't help.

"One, two, three!"

The teenager in front of them broke out into a run and cannonballed into the air, then dropped ominously beneath the cliff's edge and out of sight. Everyone in line peered over the red rocks as he splashed and anxiously held their breath, waiting for him to resurface. The boy's head popped out of the light tide, and he whooped triumphantly.

And then it was their turn. Emi stood rigid, eyes wide, legs locked.

"Josh, I'm scared," she whispered. He turned to her and took her hand.

"You're with me. Everything is fine. It's totally safe, and we are going to remember this forever. Anyway, we'd better risk our lives now before I get you knocked up," he said with a smile.

"You sure it's okay?"

"Yes. I promise," he said steadily. "Tell me when you're ready."

She took in a deep breath. "I'm ready."

"Don't let go."

He squeezed Emi's hand. They sprinted in step with each other, closer and closer to the edge, and then sprang off with all their might into the wide, open air.

In a heartbeat, they were falling. Josh held her hand the whole way, not letting go even as they crashed into the water.

CHAPTER THIRTEEN

Emi's soul seemed to float above her body as she watched herself and Josh sitting on the hospital bed, heads bowed as if in prayer.

She cradled a tiny pink bundle. Though Josh's arms were wrapped around her tightly, Emi couldn't stop herself from shaking uncontrollably.

Her lip wobbled, and heavy tears splashed on the baby's blanket. A toxic mixture of fear, sadness, worry, and dread rushed through her like the flooding of a dam, overflowing her veins and filling her lungs. She was in pure panic. Not for her own life, but much, much worse.

"What do you mean she's not breathing? Isn't she breathing now?" she pleaded, looking up through watery, blurred vision.

"Yes," the doctor said. "She is." Emi could barely make out her tight hair bun and white coat. "However, her body isn't taking in oxygen like it should. Can you see she has a bit of a blue tint around her lips?"

Emi glanced down, but the crying made it impossible to see. She wiped her wet cheek on her shoulder, staring desperately at her baby slumbering in her arms.

How could this be? She looks so peaceful and perfect.

"Usually, we see this in preterm babies, but since Violet was gestationally forty-one weeks and full-term, we don't have an easy explanation. And that means we don't know if the problem is something she will grow out of or if it is more serious. So, to rule everything out, we will do every test to get you those answers."

"What are you testing her for?" Josh asked.

"We will start with her heart to see if there are any holes. From there, we will check her brain and then the rest of her major organs. While we are doing those, we will send her blood to the lab to search for infection."

"Is she going to die?" The unthinkable word forced its way out of Emi in a sob.

The doctor cleared her throat. "I don't think so. It is a possibility, which is why we are moving her to the NICU room. But let's not get ahead of ourselves. We will take every precaution and great care of baby Violet while we try to find out why this is happening. We would like to start by taking her for a heart echocardiogram. Would you like a few minutes to discuss?"

"We don't need a discussion," Josh said with authority. "Whatever Violet needs is what we will do. And we defer to the hospital's expertise. We would, however, appreciate a moment to ourselves."

The doctor took Violet from Emi's grip.

They kissed her fuzzy little head and dimpled hands, and then the doctor laid Violet in the covered infant cart, filling her lungs with pumped oxygen, and pushed her silently out of the room.

Only then did Emi look at Josh. Though he was always such a calming force for her and had been so assertive and strong with the doctor, his face sank when he met her eyes. Suddenly, Josh looked like a little boy, small and meek in an oversized world.

"I'm sorry," he said with a hung head. "I couldn't fix it. I'm so sorry."

"What?" Emi asked, bewildered.

"I'm supposed to be able to fix anything. I'm a husband and a father now. That's my job."

This time, Emi pulled him into her, and he cried in her arms for once. And through their shared terror, she realized she never felt closer to him.

"It's your turn," Josh groaned.

Lightning cracked and lit up the window, silhouetting the tree line in the distance. The wind whipped around the little house, and thunder rumbled the ground.

"My turn? Fuck that. It's four in the morning. I've been up with him since two-thirty. I literally just got back in bed," Emi said desperately.

"I have to go to work in a few hours," Josh said, stuffing his head under his pillow.

"Oh, I don't work? You try staying home with two little kids all day," she spat back. "How about this? I'll go to work, and you can get everyone up and dressed and to school, clean up the house, go grocery shopping, do laundry, dinner, bathtime, and bedtime."

Emi softened her tone to speak to the bundle of covers between them.

"Jack, sweetheart. Come on, I'll take you back to bed." She sat up and pulled on the two little upside-down toddler legs sticking out of the comforter.

"I'm scared!" Jack petitioned. "Mamma, I'm scared!"

Another crack of thunder sent him further under the sheets.

"I know, honey. I'll come snuggle."

Satisfied, Jack sat up and held out his arms. Emi picked him up, and he wrapped himself around her. She wobbled in the pitch-black room but found her footing.

The bedroom door opened and the hall nightlight illuminated the daisies on Violet's favorite nightgown as she rubbed her eyes in the doorway. "Mommy?"

She squealed in fear as the house lit up from another lightning shot, throwing Emi's shadow on the wall. Vi sprinted in the dark toward her.

"It's okay, sweetheart," Emi said as she picked her up with her free arm, repositioning Jack so she could carry a child on each hip.

When she returned to the room forty-five minutes later, Josh rolled over and put his hand on her arm as she crawled back into the haven of her bed.

"This fucking sucks," he said softly.

They sat on the large terrace of their suite, overlooking the turquoise waves of the Caribbean as the sun set orange and pink in the distance.

"If this isn't the best way to end a day," Emi said, sighing, "I don't know what is."

"Are you happy?" Josh asked, pouring champagne into flutes and handing one to her.

"Do you have to ask me that? I am the happiest girl in the world. What more could I ask for?" She smiled.

"Good," he said. "That's all I ever want. For you to be happy." Josh picked up her hand and kissed it. "I love you more than you'll ever know, Emelie Collette Felice."

They clinked their glasses together.

"Happy ten years. It's truly been the best decade of my life," he said with a smile.

"Josh, there is one thing that could make me happier."

"I think I know what it is. I have been thinking the same thing, actually."

"Really? I just haven't had the time or the energy, honestly. But now that the kids are getting bigger, and we're done having babies . . ." Emi trailed off. "What? Why are you looking at me like that?"

"I'm just confused, is all. Go on."

"You don't think I should start writing again?"

"Oh, well. No, of course." He cleared his throat. "I just thought you were going to say something different."

"What did you think I was going to say?"

"I was hoping we might have one more." He shrugged.

"One more what?"

"Baby, silly. Three seems like such a good number to me."

"Well, I just hadn't thought about it, I guess," Emi stammered. "But, what about us? This is the first trip without the kids since our honeymoon. And I thought we were talking about traveling more. Josh, we'd have to start all over again."

More specifically, I will have to start all over again.

Anxiety hit her as forty pounds of pregnancy, sleepless newborn nights, postpartum depression, breastfeeding, bottles and diapers, colic, and all the worry and stress that came with loving and caring for another helpless being flashed before her.

I'm just finding myself again. And he wants me to jump right back into the frying pan?

"No, it's okay. I get it," Josh said, deflated. Emi couldn't stand to see him so sad. "I just don't want us to look back and have any regrets, you know?"

Damn it. No wonder he's such a good lawyer. He always knows just what to say. She could feel her conviction waning.

"Let's just put a pin in it for now, and you promise to think about it?" he asked, booping her nose. Josh brought her close and began kissing her neck up and down. "But you know, we would need a bigger house. The big white one on that street you love is still for sale."

"The brick one with the black shutters?"

"And the cherry tree."

CHAPTER FOURTEEN

2022

Vanilla clouds hung like cotton candy against the bright blue sky. Emi giggled as she tried her best to keep up, but her little legs were no match for her small friend's brilliant wings.

"Wait for me!" she called as it soared out of sight.

Emi dropped the flowers she had been picking and skipped through the grassy clearing, searching the canopy of tall evergreens for a shock of bright blue. Bees buzzed happily in the pink and purple wildflowers, and the creek babbled noisily in the woods. Emi rounded a bend and could just make out the inviting sight of the lake house's pitched roof and red siding through the trees.

Giggling in their Steelers jerseys and cutoff shorts, the gang of girlfriends slipped through the sea of black and gold to cross the Roberto Clemente Bridge, White Claws in hand.

For as long as Emi could remember, every street in the North Shore was blocked off during game day, allowing throngs of Pittsburghers to make their way to pray at the altar of Heinz Field for Sunday Football.

"Starting in sixth grade, our parents would give us two tickets and one twenty-dollar bill and drop us off on the other side of the bridge," Emi said.

"Can you imagine?" Lauren squawked.

"I don't know, it was the nineties," Emi joked.

"Even with babies and life, we've managed to make it to a game every year, no matter what," Fae added, a wistful look on her face as she considered the dark water shimmering beneath them. "Remember when we brought Zoe when she was a baby? I think she was like five or six months old."

"Start 'em young," Emi said with a grin.

Lauren opened her purse and pulled out a little plastic baggie. "Well, no babies today. Anyone else want a gummy?"

"Oh, me!" Emi answered excitedly. "Are they the ones you had last time?"

"No, these aren't as strong."

"Thank God." Emi whistled. "I was high for hours. Seriously! My whole body was tingling, even my vagina."

"I want some of that! I'm overdue for a vagina tingle, let me tell you," Fae said with a grin.

Everyone laughed as Emi popped a small piece of candy in her mouth and passed the bag along.

It was a quick walk to the stadium. They made it to their seats, oversized drinks in one hand and cardboard boxes of junk food in the other. The national anthem belted out, and then Pittsburgh quickly got down to the business of its high-stakes rivalry.

The entire city had come out for the contentious match, leaving not one empty seat in the arena. Boats bobbed on the riverfront to watch the game, and every steel bridge leading to downtown was lined with fans.

"Holy shit, it's hot on this side. There's zero shade," Lauren complained. "My underboobs are sweating already. Can you see?" She stuck her chest out for Fae to look.

"No, not yet." Fae picked up her Terrible Towel and wiped it across her forehead. "Jesus. I'm sweating out those tequila shots from last night. I thought it was supposed to be fall?"

"There is no more fall anymore. Just dead-ass summer and apocalyptic winter," Emi sniped, holding up her empty can. "I'm going for another. Anyone else need one?"

She ran for shade and weaved quickly through a barrage of fans. As she joined a lengthy queue of thirsty patrons at the bar cart, Emi winced at the New England Patriots' jerseys littered throughout the line, amused by her inherited disdain.

Her gaze fell upon a little girl on her daddy's shoulders, wearing a pair of blue fairy wings. The bluebird from the night before flashed in Emi's mind, her tiny dream-fingers outstretched, trying to touch it.

But a collective gasp interrupted Emi's vision. She looked at the nearby TV screen to watch the game, holding her breath as Trubisky chucked the ball in slow motion toward the endzone. As it soared midair for two painstaking seconds, spectators and players alike rose to their feet, slack-jawed in the hope of a connection.

The concrete walls and ceiling shook with the stomping and roaring of sixty-five thousand fans. Touchdown.

Strangers whooped and high-fived, and Emi had just broken into her running man victory dance when someone tapped her shoulder. The hair on her neck stood at attention as an odd feeling crept over her. It was like she was watching a movie she had seen a hundred times before, and yet, for the first time.

A deep voice cut through the air behind her.

"Emi?" Jesse said.

CHAPTER FIFTEEN

Jesse

They stood there, searching each other. Except for his pounding heart, Jesse lost all feeling. Everyone and everything around them stopped, frozen in time.

Before he knew it, Jesse opened his arms wide and scooped her up. Her body felt so right next to his. As her delicate fingers rested on his shoulders, she slipped her head into the curve of his neck. He closed his eyes and breathed in her sweet floral smell.

Just like that, he was swept away by the tide. Glimpses of his hands on her body and her whispers in his ears rushed him. They were making love on a creaky wooden floor next to a fire, Christmas stockings hung on a hearth. A small ring sparkled from Emi's left hand. Snow fell silently beyond old windows with chipped paint. As their bodies moved together, a hand in her long, soft hair, the fit between them was tailor-made. She completed him.

But his daydream was dashed as Emi suddenly ran cold, and she pulled out of his arms. Real life and her disappointment in him had brought her back. She dropped from his embrace and stepped away. Betrayal flashed red-hot in her eyes, crushing him like a mallet.

This is it. Go big or go home.

"I was hoping you might be here," he said. "Emi, I'm so sorry. I know I should have shown up to the diner."

"It's whatever," she spat, but her voice was pure ice.

"You don't understand," Jesse said.

"I don't need to." Emi turned away from him and crossed her arms. "It's not like we were ever really friends or anything."

She knew exactly what to say to impale him.

"Can I explain?" he asked. Emi still wouldn't face him, but she didn't walk away.

Jesse took a deep breath. It was now or never. Maybe for the first time in his life, he had to find the courage to be completely and totally vulnerable.

"I did go," he said, hanging his head. "I saw you waiting for me, and I just panicked. You looked so beautiful sitting there, but something kept me from opening the door. I wanted to, I really wanted to."

Emi's shoulders slumped. "I don't get it, Jesse. It was just lunch—which happened to be your idea, by the way. And not only did you stand me up, you ghosted me."

"I did, but not because I don't care. Because I'm an immature idiot who doesn't know how to deal with my feelings," Jesse admitted.

Emi slowly turned around, and he took that as a sign to keep going. Jesse reached into his pocket and pulled out a small, frayed black hair tie. Taking a deep breath, he held it out so she could see.

"You're right, we aren't really friends," he said. "We only knew each other for three seconds decades ago. But I've thought about you, in some way, every day since."

She looked at the small oval in his open hand, her eyes as large and mesmerizing as the moon. Emi carefully took the decades-old relic and folded it over in her hands.

"Is this . . . ?" He nodded. "How?"

"I went back for it the next day."

"And you've kept it all this time?" Emi whispered.

"Before you freak out, I know you're married. I know you have a beautiful family, and I'm happy for you. I want you to have a happy life. Truly. I would never jeopardize that. It's just that running into you brought up so many things that I had let go of. And, honestly, Emi, I just didn't think I could be with you again and look you in those big brown eyes of yours."

She let him graze her cheek with his fingers. "I couldn't pretend to want to leave it at lunch."

The anger had dissolved from Emi's face.

"I'm sorry. I'm really, really sorry. The last thing I ever wanted was to hurt you or make you feel rejected in any way," he swore. "I could never reject you. To me, you are everything. I've never felt about anyone the way I feel about you. I had no clue, at twenty-two, what to do about it. And at forty-one, I still don't. I regret every second I didn't tell you how I feel. If I could do it all over again, I would do everything differently. But I can't. I know that.

But just please, don't hate me, Emi. I have to live with my regrets, but I don't think I could live with that, too."

Jesse thought he saw a glint of wetness in her eyes. Seconds stretched between them, muted by the noise of seventy-five thousand fans cheering and stomping as the Steelers pulled off another play. But though their bodies stood amongst the chaos of the game, the two of them were stuck fast, like stone statues under a spell.

Emi
"Ma'am. Ma'am," a woman behind the counter fussed at her, annoyed. The spell broke.

Emi's face turned red. "Oh. Sorry," she said sheepishly as she stepped toward the bar cart, realizing they were holding up the line. "Three black cherry White Claws, please."

She reached into her pocket to pull out her credit card, but Jesse stepped in front of her.

"It's on me. Can we sit down for a second? I won't keep you long, promise." He nodded at an empty bench nearby and helped her carry the drinks over.

"You know, I've never really put myself out there like that. I hope I didn't freak you out. I swear I'm not a stalker or anything."

"No, it was really brave of you." She sighed. "I'm not freaked out. I think I'm just sad," she said as she fidgeted in her seat. "I mean." She cleared her throat. "I feel the same way you do."

Emi peered into Jesse's dark eyes and found something so real, so genuine. She forced herself to look away before she was lost forever.

The little girl in the blue wings held her daddy's hand as she walked past, licking an ice-cream cone. All the signs, dreams, and coincidences Emi had experienced over the last few months came flooding back, covering her body in goosebumps.

"I'm in town until Tuesday. Will you meet me tonight, or tomorrow even? Just as friends. I'll go anywhere. You tell me. I want to make it up to you. I'll do anything."

"I would love that."

Emi wanted nothing else but to meet him again. That night, the next day, and every other day for the rest of their lives.

"But I can't." It was excruciating to watch his heart collapse. "You know I can't. For all the same reasons that you didn't show up at the diner. It just wouldn't be right."

"I know." This time, he looked away. "I've tried since we met twenty years ago. But I can't promise I won't think about you anymore."

Emi broke in two.

"Same," she said. "I can't say anything else because there's a line I won't cross. But I feel the same."

I wish I could tell him so much more.

But his eyes told her she didn't have to. He knew already.

They stood and held each other too close. She rested her head on his chest, and he nuzzled her deeper. Emi closed her eyes and felt his nose in her hair. A tear rolled down her cheek, and an image came to her as clear as day.

He held her in a joyful embrace at the end of a stone pathway at twilight. Luminaries and fireflies lit the faces of their loved ones as they clapped. Her dress was made of silk, and never in her entire life had she felt more loved.

"I guess some things just aren't meant to be," Jesse said. Emi took a step back and looked at him. The words surprised her as they came out of her mouth.

"Maybe in our next life."

Emi threw herself into a bathroom stall just before the tears came. She sat on the toilet, put her head in her hands, and cried.

She loved Josh and the kids. It was a fundamental truth that she would rather die than hurt them. But as blessed as she was, life could still feel so cruel sometimes.

Her feelings for Jesse were mutual. He had loved her in secret this whole time, from hundreds of miles away. Every time she suppressed a thought about him over the years, so did he. And instead of making her feel better, it made everything worse.

So, she cried. Because she felt, even being in his arms for just a few moments, what could have been all along. And every cell in her body screamed to go back.

They had been so young, so stupid. They had both been too immature to be vulnerable. She had subscribed to the dumb gender ideology myth that the boy was supposed to chase her and that if he didn't, it meant he didn't want to.

Now here they were. And the truth was that this information changed nothing. Emi was still sentenced to wonder forever, in silent heartache, where life might have taken her.

If only.

"Emi?" Fae's voice echoed in the bathroom. "Are you in here?"

"I'm here," Emi said, wiping her eyes.

"I got your text. Are you okay?"

Emi swung the stall door open, and Fae gasped at her tear-streaked face.

"What happened? What's wrong?"

"I need to leave. Can we leave? I'm sorry," Emi croaked. "I just want to go home."

They left right then and there. Fae texted their girlfriends an excuse and walked Emi the half mile back to the car. The world was a blur. Mesmerized by the weed gummy and stunning events of the day, Emi was quiet all the way down the stadium ramp, across the sea of parking lots, and back over the bridge. It was only once she was safely in Fae's small Honda that, halfway home, she spoke again.

"Are you sure you don't want to sleep over again? It's not a problem," Fae said as she pulled her car onto Emi's street. "My mom will keep the girls another night. We'll watch your favorites and sleep in."

"No, that's okay. Honestly, I just want to take a hot bath and crawl into my bed."

"What will you tell Josh?" Fae asked. Emi wiped her eyes.

"I'll just tell him I'm sick or that I have a headache or something. It'll be fine."

Fae frowned. "I'm just surprised you never told me this before."

"What do you mean? I've told you everything since I bumped into him on my birthday."

"No, I mean how you've felt about him for the last twenty years. I guess I kind of knew anyway. And I don't expect you to tell me everything. It just breaks my heart that you've been so sad all alone."

"I know I can tell you anything, Fae. I think I didn't want to admit my feelings to myself. Because if I said it out loud, I would have to deal with them, you know?"

"Yeah, honey, I do."

"Something he said bothers me, though," Emi murmured.

"What's that?"

"He said he was hoping I'd be at the game today. What are the odds that we would be in the same stadium, at the same football game, with that many people, and we would bump into each other? Do you think he knew I'd be there?" She shook her head. "There's no way he could have known."

"Well," Fae said cautiously. "I have an idea how he could have. When a couple of the girls said they couldn't make it today, I tagged you in that post I made on Facebook about selling their tickets. Remember?"

"Yeah," Emi said, suddenly feeling very suspicious.

"Well, I may have accidentally made it public. And it literally mapped out exactly where our seats were." Fae swallowed. "And it may not have been an accident."

Understanding washed over Emi as she let herself sink into the seat.

"I'm sorry, Emi. You were so sad, and he needed to make it better. So, I just sprinkled a little information out to the Universe so he could step up and fix it. I had no idea he would actually go. I mean, that flight from Colorado is what, six hours?"

Emi nodded to herself, processing all her feelings. She may have never loved or been annoyed with Fae more.

"So, you're really not going to meet up with him before he leaves town?"

"Seeing him again only makes everything worse. No, I have to cut him off and move on. For everyone's sake."

"I understand, honey," she said, mirroring Emi's grief. "This is going to sound trite, but I genuinely believe that things happen for a reason. You wouldn't be who you are now if you had been with Jesse. You would've been a whole other person. Maybe we wouldn't have stayed as close. Maybe you wouldn't have your kids. Who knows, you could have been a heroin addict or—worse—a Ravens fan."

"Never," Emi said, breaking a smile. "In none of my lives would I ever be anything but a Steelers girl."

Fae laughed. "Josh and the kids are so lucky to have you. Honestly, Em, I don't know how many other people could walk away from a Primary Soulmate."

Emi didn't object. It was precisely how she felt. Jesse completed her in some cosmic way, like a large piece of her soul was out there in the wide world, walking around without her.

"Get some sleep, honey. Even broken hearts feel better in the morning."

Emi woke to the door creaking open. A beam of light cut through the darkened room and shot across the floor.

"Emi?" Josh called gently.

She heard his soft footsteps and felt his weight sit atop the goose-down comforter she had tunneled into. Emi rubbed her swollen eyes, her lashes still damp and stuck together from a long night of crying.

"What happened? You've been in bed for hours. Is everything okay?"

Emi cleared her throat and sat up to face her worried husband. "Yeah, I'm sorry. I just have a terrible headache. It must have been the gummy I ate, maybe. Thanks for letting me sleep."

"Sure. Did you have fun at the game?"

"Yes, but I didn't feel good, so Fae had to bring me home in the fourth quarter."

Emi couldn't meet his eyes, fearing he might see through all her lies. Josh was peering into her face, studying her like he was trying to decipher a coded message.

"Hey," he said. "I wanted to talk to you about something."

Shit. Does he know?

"I feel like maybe you've been unhappy lately. Like, with us," he continued. "No, please don't say anything. Just let me talk first.

I get that our lives haven't been as exciting as you might have hoped they would be. We had all these dreams, and then life, kids, and my career just kind of took over. For you more than me. I know my work is a lot. And that leaves you in the lurch with all the responsibility of our home life. It's totally overwhelming, and I see that.

But I don't know. It feels like maybe you've been drifting from me a little bit, too. I just want to say that I love you endlessly, and I will do whatever I need to do to bring you back."

Well, I am just the worst fucking person on the entire planet. Josh is so sweet and loving—and I'm crying over someone else.

"Honey, I'm sorry. I have been a little distant, I guess. It's nothing you did, it's me."

"I know I'm not the best at anticipating your needs. I get sidetracked easily, and I don't always do the greatest job of giving you the attention you deserve."

Clearly, it's me who doesn't deserve you.

"No, Josh," Emi said. "It's okay."

"No, it's not. I know how frustrating I can be sometimes because I don't pick up on a lot of things. I can be really daft, and you're so much more intelligent and thoughtful than I am. But I want you to know that I'm going to try harder." His voice cracked with emotion. "I also want you to know that even though we have a lot of differences, they're what I love the most about us."

"What, you love that we don't understand each other?"

"I love that you challenge me to think outside of my comfort zone. You force me to be more empathetic and see things differently. I've grown so much as a person because of you. I'm a better father and a better man. And I love that you're so fun and keep me guessing. I would be bored out of my mind if I had ended up with anyone else."

She gave him a little smile. "Yeah, I get that. I'm a better person because of you, too," Emi said, putting her hand on his. "And you could not be a greater husband if you tried. Sometimes, Josh, I just feel so—I don't know—flawed? Dull? Stagnant? Insecure? All the things, I guess. But somehow, you always see the best in me. Thank you."

"All of that is normal, Em. And you see the best in me, too." He was right. She did.

"You're never going to be perfect, hun. And neither will I. But all I've ever cared about is making you smile. I'll do anything for you to be happy with me again."

"Josh, I am happy."

She put her arms around him and hugged him tightly.

This man is the epitome of unconditional love. How can I want anything else?

As they lay down together for the night, Emi let Josh wrap his arms around her and pull her close. It was time, really time, to finally let go of Jesse. And no matter what the twenty-one-year-old still living inside her wanted, he had been right. Some things just weren't meant to be.

One last tear rolled down her cheek, and Jesse's eyes, dark and defeated, came to her as she closed her own.

CHAPTER SIXTEEN

A brilliant spot of blue erupted from a treetop and into the sky.

"Wait for me!" she squealed. Emi dropped the flowers she had been picking and ran out of the forest, following the bluebird into her backyard, where it chirped at her from a small apple tree. Beyond it lay a charming red cottage. In the distance, Chautauqua Lake glistened like diamonds while white sailboats bobbed lazily on its surface.

The bluebird jumped off its branch and hopped through the flower bed, pausing long enough to tease her outstretched fingers. Black-eyed Susans were bursting all around her, and she frolicked past the large hydrangea bushes on the side of the little house, the bird leading the way.

It landed on the roof of the front porch, and Emi's small feet skipped up the broad stone steps, where her big sister sat happily, holding two giant popsicles. Rosie smiled at Emi, and suddenly, she was very aware of her long, wild locks. She envied her sister's tight, strawberry-blond French braids because, unlike her, Rosie was always tidy and put together.

Emi hopped onto the porch swing next to her and lit up with delight as Rosie nudged one of the popsicles her way. The girls' tabby cat slinked through the front door and into the garden, off to chase frogs in the marsh by the lake.

Rosie licked her sweet treat carefully as Emi stained her lips and chin red, getting an astonishing amount on her face. Once every bit had been devoured and the wooden stick sucked dry, Emi wiped herself off with the back of her hand, then looked at her sister with a contented sigh.

But Rosie wasn't so little anymore. In the blink of an eye, she'd shifted into her forty-three-year-old self, which seemed to Emi perfectly natural and not alarming in the least. Her own forty-year-old legs were long enough to feel the scratchy fibers of the outdoor rug beneath them.

"Oh my God," she said, recognizing the music drifting through the open living room window. "Loggins and Messina. Mom used to love "Danny's Song." What's she doing in there?"

"She's cooking dinner. Roast chicken and potatoes, your favorite. Can you hear her singing?"

They stopped to listen, giggling at their mother's voice.

"What are we doing here? Am I dreaming?"

"Not exactly. You are sleeping but not quite dreaming—not in the way you mean, anyway. I asked you to meet me here. We're in one of your favorite memories."

"One of my memories?"

"Yep. Dad will go into the kitchen in a minute, and they'll start singing and dancing together. Remember?"

Just as Rosie said, their father's voice met their mother's in song. The girls joined in, and Rosie kicked the ground happily with one foot, swinging them gently back and forth. When she picked her own off the ground, she witnessed her seven-year-old toes again, bare and dirty from a day of hide-and-seek outside.

Emi felt nothing but love and gratitude, happiness and belonging. She was safe with her family, and in this moment, her young life was sweet perfection, untarnished by time and experience, brimming with innocence and possibility.

"This memory is so special to me."

"You've held it sacred your whole life. It helped influence your marriage and, in turn, helped your kids."

"How's that?"

"Because you've passed on just as much love and stability as you felt in this moment, and you'll keep it with you forever."

"That's nice," Emi said with a smile. "Rosie, you said you asked me to meet you here. What does that mean?"

She took a deep breath and cleared her throat. They were adults once more.

"My consciousness, which is the part of my soul that is aware of my experiences, asked your consciousness to meet here while the remaining parts of us are sleeping. I'm your most trusted person in this lifetime, so I asked you to pick one of your favorite memories of the two of us. And I have to say, this is a good one."

"Wait. Where is here? Like, are we in my brain or something?"

"Your soul left your body on autopilot while you are in a different dimension. The dimension of memory." Before Emi could interject, she continued. "You're at a fork in the road, baby sister. You've learned lessons and ascended to a new vibrational plane. And I have an opportunity for you."

Emi furrowed her brow. "What lessons were learned? I don't follow."

"The scenario at the football game was designed as a turning point for you. You could have chosen to leave your life for Jesse, who is your eternal love, or stay with Josh, who is your life's love and happiness. You chose to stay with your husband, even though you've been dreaming about the moment you and Jesse might confess your feelings for each other since the first night you met in college."

"So, this was all some fucked-up test? What is breaking my heart like this supposed to teach me?"

"No, it's not a test. It was an option. In your previous incarnation, the two of you were happily married. Until Jesse went off script and allowed the challenges of life to overcome him. He ran from his feelings and, in turn, from you, too. You allowed his choices to overshadow the remainder of your life and never moved on, and you died devastated and alone. But this time," Rosie said proudly, "you chose yourself. Not only have you healed your karma of disregarding your past life's worth and joy, but you have also protected your family from the lifetime of hurt and trauma choosing Jesse would have brought upon them. Turning your back on such a strong interdimensional relationship for any reason is more than challenging, but you did it."

Emi stared blankly at her.

"Before I can tell you more, I have to explain some things so you can understand. And I'm a die-hard skeptic, so you know what I'm telling you is accurate."

"Rose, spit it out already."

"Let me ask you a question. What do you think this whole life thing is about?"

"Love. I think it's about love," Emi said.

Rose nodded. "We incarnate onto this planet to learn about humanity, love, and our fallible emotions through firsthand experiences. We learn that everything we do affects us and others, and in turn, everything others do affects us. We feel all the good, the bad, and the in-between, which is what being human truly means."

"Okay, sure." Emi snorted. "Whatever you say, Rose."

"I'm serious. Before being born as Emelie Collette Klein, you were, first and foremost, a soul. You are your own consciousness in a larger collective consciousness. After this life, your soul will rewatch Emelie's journey from start to finish in the third person, observing it from afar, and learn from it differently, with an outside perspective."

Emi knew she looked perplexed, and Rosie elaborated.

"The Master Realm is our eternal home. And there, we live, evolve, and even go to school to help us learn and grow. When we're ready, we take field trips to Earth to learn through experience and choice. Then, when it's all over, we return to the classroom to discuss what happened.

When you were last in your classroom, you chose to be Emi Klein. Your soul liked the exposure of traveling internationally as a child and being a part of a nuclear family."

Emi recalled her visions of the crowded ship and her father's shoulders, of Jesse's Coptic cross and their son's bright smile. "How many lives have I had?"

"Thousands."

"What happened to the memories of all of the other ones, then?"

"You'll remember them fully in the Master Realm. You have done wonderful things and terrible things in your many lives."

"Why are we taking these classes in the first place?" Emi asked, her mind working hard. "When I took classes in college, it was to graduate so that I could get a good job and live a comfortable life. What's the end game?"

"To get closer to God."

"So there really is a God? Shit, I swear a lot. And like, I definitely had sex before marriage, and still drink and eat gummies, and—"

"No, Emi," Rosie laughed. "God doesn't care about those things. It doesn't care what religion we are or that you stole those twenty dollars from my piggy bank in fourth grade."

"Oh my God, I told you I didn't take your stupid money, Rose," Emi protested, but Rosie just grinned.

"None of those things are important. It's whether you're a good person that matters most. Are you kind, fair, and genuine? Have you managed your emotions and reactions? Do you stand up for what's right, face lessons head-on, or live in fear? Fear is a biggie. But also, are you good to others and to yourself? It's that last part, the 'being good to yourself' part, that you've been working on lately." Rosie paused to let her words percolate. "But I can't give you all of life's secrets. That just wouldn't be fair. And anyway, we need to talk about time."

"Time?"

"Time is not consecutive. It's concurrent." Rosie laughed as Emi raised an exaggerated eyebrow. "Okay, think of your life as something tangible, like a novel."

Emi blinked and found herself sitting at a desk in a gold, shimmery classroom. A teacher, veiled in iridescent blue sparkles, stood lecturing at the head of a class of students in white clothing. She handed out thick books with names inscribed in silver on the front. Emi turned to Rosie at the desk next to her, who gave her a wink.

"When you sit down to read your novel," Rosie said, "the entire thing already exists. Your whole story, from start to finish, has already been written. Your life is the same way. All of it already exists when you begin to read it."

Emi fell into the pages of her open book. Rows of mercury words became three-dimensional moments of her life as she walked past.

"When you live your life, you are brought through page by page, so it feels that one moment leads to the next. But in actuality, the story is already there: prologue, arc, and ending."

Emi turned from the gigantic pages she stood on to look up at a larger version of herself in the golden classroom, who was still reading the book, watching her smaller self as she went.

"It's quite fascinating. All of it is designed to happen in such a way that your human brain can make sense of it and hopefully learn about your actions and their consequences. And, of course, your soul's journey doesn't end at death—just your incarnated lifetime."

Emi opened her desk to find it had no bottom, just an ever-expanding stack of many colored books, all inscribed with different names. There were short books, fat books, and hard and soft covers.

And then they were back on the porch swing.

"But if everything already exists, is free will just an illusion? Were all my choices already decided for me before I was born? Like, am I just moving through the Matrix, following some predetermined story?"

"It's both. Some things are fated, and you can't change them, but a lot of the story can be modified during life. And even if you're fated for something, you can still reconstruct your destiny, which is how you get there. Everybody has free will, and there is practically no life that doesn't have some kind of deviation from the plan they incarnated with."

"If I wrote my life before I was born but choose to stray from the plan while I'm living, what happens?"

"If it affects your story in a major way, another reality is instantly created. A new dimension is born with the same exact characters, scenes, and backstory as the original, containing a carbon copy of the chapters until the page, paragraph, and word you choose to depart from. You essentially make another edition of the first version."

"What happens to the original book?" Emi asked. "Does it just disappear into thin air?"

"No. Your new lifetime is layered next to the original, like the stack of books you saw in your desk. Each dimension with a different timeline is its own physical space, as there is the possibility of infinite realities and, therefore, infinite dimensions. And we can access these different dimensions—and the beings living in them—through thoughts and dreams."

"But how can I be in parallel dimensions at once?"

"That is a tricky question. Our souls can be split into as many pieces as we want. However, the conscious awareness of our souls—the part that recognizes what is happening, makes decisions, and learns—can only be in one place at a time. That's why when you're dreaming, you are unaware of what is going on around your physical body. Your consciousness is in the dream dimension."

Emi blinked again. When she opened her eyes this time, she lay in a comfortable bed, glowing with golden light, reading her life book. She closed the book halfway through and picked up another from her nightstand, leaving the first book in its place.

"You can't read two books at once, right? Imagine you put down *The Hunger Games* and start reading *Lord of the Rings* instead. *The Hunger Games* still exists. It doesn't end when you stop reading it or disappear because you set it aside. You've simply diverted your attention."

"Okay. I think I understand," Emi said slowly. "But how would I know if I veered from my story and made the wrong decision?"

"Well, there is no right or wrong decision because we learn lessons through every experience. But to stay in line with what you chose for yourself in the Master Realm is easy. Just listen to your intuition."

"Oh, it's that easy, huh?" Emi said sarcastically. "Like anyone even knows what intuition is. If it's even real."

"It is. You've pretty much been listening to your gut feelings your whole life."

"Like when?"

"Like when your intuition told you not to let Mikey Ryan drive you home from that party your sophomore year, even though he was the most popular guy in high school."

Emi saw herself again in her mind's eye—fifteen and skinny, with long, shiny dark hair and a dazed, drunken look. Mikey was tall with a charming smile, a backward hat, and just the right amount of late-nineties sag in his jeans.

"I'm going past your house anyway," he said, with the coercion of a snake luring prey into its trap.

"No, thanks. Really," Emi slurred from her seat on the steps outside a raging house party.

"I'm a good guy, Emi." He cockily dangled his car keys in one hand. "I'll get you home safe and sound. Promise."

Mikey took her hand and pulled her toward his car.

Something in her stomach flipped, and the hair on her neck stood straight up. Emi snatched her hand away and shook her head.

"I'm going to find Fae." And as the words came out of her mouth, she knew she was absolutely, positively not safe with him.

Back on the porch, nestled safely beside her sister, Emi's skin crawled.

"What would have happened?" she asked.

"That's not something you really need to know, though listening to yourself in that instance kept you safe. But you also followed your intuition when you marched down to Fae's house at six years old and asked her if she wanted to play."

Emmi watched as she, a young child with bouncing pigtails, skipped down the street carrying her two favorite dolls, wearing a huge, hopeful grin on her little face. She strode past a large truck and weaved through cumbersome furniture carried over a front yard by thick, sweaty movers until she got to the front door.

As she stood on her tiptoes to reach the bell, a gray cat darted onto the stairs and wrapped around her legs. A lanky girl with white-yellow hair in need of a good brushing poked her head around the open doorway.

"Hi! I'm Emi! I like your cat. What's her name?"

"Jem, from *Jem and the Holograms*," the girl said.

"I love cats! Want to start a Cat Club with me?" Emi asked.

Fae broke out into a giant, toothless grin. "I would love to!"

Emi shoved one of the dolls at her new best friend, and they both giggled as Fae pulled her inside.

"The two of you are soulmates and were meant to spend your lives together," Rosie said.

Emi perked up. "Really? I thought a soulmate was a romantic thing?"

"No way. The term means that you and someone else have made a soul contract before you came to influence each other in some way. A soulmate can show up in any relationship, including with animals. And they don't always have to play significant roles in our lives.

You recognized a soulmate of yours in the bookstore once. Do you remember when you simultaneously grabbed the same book off the shelf?"

Emi drifted into another memory. She stood in a long aisle of books, let out a yelp, and then burst into nervous laughter at the coincidence of a stranger going for the same book at the same time.

"Oh, I am so sorry! I didn't mean to take this from you," the man said and chivalrously handed her the book. As she looked into his blue eyes, her body tingled, and a serendipitous silence overtook them.

"I knew something happened. I could feel it, but I didn't know what," Emi breathed. Rosie smiled encouragingly. "How did we influence each other? We didn't even talk."

"Your souls identified each other from the deal you made in the Master Realm. And your intuition kept you on course. Instead of introducing yourself and striking up a conversation, you simply said, 'Thank you,' and walked away. But the excitement you got from how he looked at you—as if you were the most beautiful girl he had ever seen—pushed you back on course. That's when you realized you were ready to stop seeing assholes and find someone who would revere you like that forever."

"So, the Universe just . . . conjured a whole person for me? Just to give me a push?" Emi grimaced. "I'm not that special."

"You are that special—but so is everyone else. It's a two-way street; bumping into you did something for him, too. Both of your souls agreed to help nudge each other along."

"And it wasn't long after that I ran into Josh," Emi said with a quiet smile as she put together the events of her life.

"Josh is your soulmate, as well. The two of you have a very long-standing and important soul relationship. Again, you chose each other before you came. And you got together at the exact time you were supposed to. Your intuition led both of you to Walnut Street on that dark winter night. It told him to get cash out of the ATM, even though it was freezing outside and completely out of his way."

Emi watched as Josh trudged through the slushy sidewalk on a dark winter night, wrapped in a warm wool peacoat. A gust of snow fell, sparkling in the wind, as it whipped around him, reddening his nose. But as the glistening air swept away, and as if someone had called his name, Josh suddenly spun around and backtracked in his steps before stopping in front of an ATM. He looked up, eyes dancing, as a group of giggling girls, half naked in the snow, rounded the corner from down the street.

"Violet is another soulmate with whom you have spent many lives. In the life before this one, she was a mentor of yours whom you loved dearly. You asked for her to come back to you."

"Is that why I felt like I already knew her when she was born? Like, it wasn't 'nice to meet you' but more 'I'm so happy to see you again.'"

As Emi spoke the words to Rosie, she held Vi in her arms, a newborn fresh from her womb, swaddled in a pink blanket. She looked down at her daughter's face, smushed and pink, and whispered, "I remember you."

"Exactly," Rosie said. "So many of our relationships and moments are prearranged, and specific lessons are necessary for us to experience and grow from. Some of your major lessons in this life revolve around motherhood. The terror of Vi's birth complications taught you so much, as well as helping Jack process and calm his anxieties, the depression of miscarriage, and the joy of the gift of Liam, who is nothing but pure and simple."

"So why am I here, Rosie? If I'm doing such a great job learning whatever lessons the Universe wants me to know—or that I want me to know, I guess, what is this intervention all about?"

"I told you. This is a fork in the road, a chance to veer from the path laid out for you and enact your free will. You may choose to go back to a moment from long ago and rewrite your past, creating a new dimension, or to leave things as they are."

"I can go back to a moment I've already lived?"

"Yes. Humans think of time travel as getting in a spaceship and flying backward faster than the speed of light." Rose laughed at the silliness of the thought. "We're dumb. It's so much simpler than that."

"Okay, time travel? Now I know I'm dreaming."

"Will you just shut up, please!" Rosie rolled her eyes. "Now that you understand time, you can use your consciousness as a tool to skip to moments of your life that you want to experience again or alter in some way."

"But Rosie, if I'm a soul in the Greater Consciousness of Life School, in the Master Realm or whatever, why don't I know all of this already?"

"You do. Or, should I say, your soul does. You have what's called 'dimensional amnesia.' It's a fail-safe to ensure you make your decisions naturally, out of human emotion, and not out of bias or tainted motivation. Which is why, deep down, you know what I am telling you is true."

The sun over Chautauqua Lake slowly descended, and the cat slinked back up the stairs and purred her way over to the sisters. They sat silently, swaying back and forth on the swing, the smell of roast chicken and rosemary wafting through the window. Emi looked out to the expansive lake to see a few little boats seesawing their way back to shore for dinner.

"And now that we've gone over everything, it brings us to the matter at hand," Rosie said more seriously. Emi sighed, for she already knew what it was.

Jesse.

CHAPTER SEVENTEEN

The sisters walked in step across a big yellow bridge with the city skyline behind them. The river below gleamed greenish-blue in the bright light of spring.

Emi hadn't been paying much attention to where they were going, but she suddenly stopped and looked around. The neighborhood was alive with cars, songbirds, and people out jogging or walking their dogs.

"I know where we are," she said softly.

They passed in silence through a small park with a pretty fountain on the corner of Jesse's old street. His apartment building, crumbly and timeworn, seemed to light up its surroundings.

"You have a choice to make," Rose said. "You can depart from your current life, picking it up at this point in time. Or you could return to the life you are presently leading, with Josh and the kids. Either way, you will be completely unaware that any of this ever happened."

"I won't remember this dream?"

"We aren't in a dream, Em," Rosie huffed. "And that's correct; you will lose it to the dimensional amnesia. First, though, you'll get a glimpse into what your alternate life could have been like, so it's not a totally blind decision. Not everything—but just enough."

"What happens to Josh and the kids?" Emi asked, a little dumbfounded. "If I decide to go back in time and change it all? You said they won't disappear, right?"

"You will all still be there in the original dimension. That part of your soul will exist on autopilot, and all your lives will play out together as they were supposed to. Remember, it is just your consciousness that's leaving them, which is only one aspect of the soul. But keep in mind, if you channel your awareness to this new timeline, you won't have any knowledge or memory of them for the rest of your life."

"So, I would be giving them up?" Emi stopped walking. "How the fuck am I supposed to choose between an eternal soulmate and the loves of my life?" She began to panic. "Honestly, that's like tearing my heart in two. What if I make the wrong decision? Regardless of whether I remember this or not, I'd have to live with that until I die."

"I already told you," Rosie huffed. "There is no wrong decision, Em. And yeah, it's a big choice. That's why you are getting this opportunity to see for yourself." She began to walk, and Emi followed suit. "But here's the catch: Jesse has been awarded the exact same opportunity."

"What lesson did he learn?" Emi asked, intrigued.

"Bravery for the sake of love—especially love that may not be returned. Instead of hiding from everything that scares him, afraid of making himself out to be a fool, Jesse leaned in for himself and for you. He showed restraint and respect for your life by walking away from the diner, but still confessed everything he had been holding back, knowing there was no chance of riding off into the sunset with you.

Since both of your lives—and, thus, your soul lessons—could irrevocably change from here on out, it has to be a mutual decision to rewrite your history. If you don't agree, both your lives stay as they are."

"Rosie, how can we make that decision together if we can't talk about it?"

"Oh, you absolutely have to talk about it," Rosie said with a wink.

Emi's heart skipped a beat. A tingle swept up her spine as she turned around.

"Holy shit, you're here, too?" Jesse said with wonder, presumably just as shocked to see her as she was to see him.

Emi was locked in on Jesse's burning expression, unable to turn away. The way he looked at her was so intense, and it was a few moments before anyone spoke.

"God, get a room," said a woman with Jesse's same smile, stepping from behind him and into Emi's view. The tension was cut with laughter.

"Emi, this is Jenna, my sister."

"It's so nice to meet you," Emi said. "This is my sister, Rose."

Rose and Jenna acknowledged each other with a warm smile, and once everyone was acquainted, Jesse and Emi drew back together as if pulled by a string.

"Is this real?" Emi asked him, feeling her voice tremble.

"I don't know, but even if it isn't, it's pretty fucking cool," he said as a smile crept across his face. "So, what now?"

"Walk across the street and into your apartment building. Go down the hallway and through your old door. The moment you open it, you will be living, feeling, and experiencing moments of what could have been as the present," Jenna directed him.

As if they had practiced their spiel, Rosie picked up where she left off. "You will move quickly from one point to the next until you've reached the same age that you are in your current lives. Once it's over, the two of you will be given all the time you need to talk."

"What happens once we've chosen?" Jesse asked. "Do we need to tell someone?"

"No. You'll both simply wake up, potentially in the same bed. And none of us will remember any of this. Life will just seem to be as if it always was. Are you ready?" Rosie asked, squeezing Emi's arm.

"Ready," Emi and Jesse answered in unison.

He reached out and took her hand in his as they slowly walked across the street. The old building was almost as Emi remembered it, but there was a warmth that had never existed before; it was no longer gray and drab but cast in a golden hue.

Jesse held the front door open and guided her past the wall of mailbox slots, then up the staircase to his old hallway. But where there had once been rows of apartment doors lining both sides of the long corridor, there was only one at the very end where his apartment used to be. A white glow pulsed rhythmically behind it, drawing them closer.

"I guess we know where to go, then," Emi said with a shrug and a smile, trying to break the tension.

They stood in front of the simple door, considering what was waiting for them on the other side.

Emi could feel it held so much behind it. Jesse stepped in front of her protectively, turned the old brass doorknob, and pushed.

CHAPTER EIGHTEEN

2003

The tectonic plates under her platformed feet shifted, and she almost lost her balance. A shudder washed through her. In her bones, Emi knew something had happened. She was as sure of it as she was of the chilly air in the drafty apartment—and the thin wooden door in front of her.

She held up a smooth hand with gawdy silver rings and chipped pink polish and pushed it open.

The dim apartment hallway was empty and still, begging for her to turn around and crawl back under the warm covers from which she came.

Her long locks were crunchy with day-old hairspray, and goosebumps cascaded down the sliver of exposed stomach between her crop top and low-rise jeans. She was shaky and hungover from a long night of drinking, but it wasn't just the liquor that was depressing her. Each step away from Jesse's apartment deepened her frown.

Emi reached the vestibule and stopped long enough to throw on the oversized hoodie he had chivalrously offered her to wear home. She slipped it over her head and breathed in his warm and cozy scent, like twinkling lights on a Christmas tree.

She willed Jesse to chase after her like Prince Charming, clutching a glass slipper. But when she glanced over her shoulder, hope fell as the hallway was still dark and deserted.

Emi lingered as she debated what to do. Humiliation told her to run home to the safety of Fae and her couch and never look back, but her heart begged to slip into Jesse's bed and try that morning all over again.

She had slept over the night before, and only ten minutes ago, his tongue grazed her teeth in a cringy, fumbled kiss. She shuddered.

Could I have made that any worse if I tried? Probably not.

Mortified, she reluctantly pushed the door open and stepped into the bright morning. To Emi's astonishment, the very same bluebird that sabotaged what could have been the start of something amazing sat innocently on the hood of her car as if waiting for a ride.

"Why did you do that? You ruined everything," she said to the bird, exasperated. Not really expecting an answer, it gave her pause when it cocked its head as if to say, *If you leave, you'll regret it forever.*

Prickles of understanding spread through her.

"God damn it."

Emi's obstinacy finally broke, acquiescing to the brighter voice inside. She turned on a dime and allowed her feet to carry her swiftly back so she couldn't think twice and make a run for it. The next thing she knew, she was rapping on his door.

Maybe he won't open it. What the hell am I doing? I don't even know what to say. I should just—

It swung open, and Jesse stood in front of her, still in pajamas.

"I'm sorry, I think I forgot something," Emi said. Then, forcing herself not to chicken out, she grabbed Jesse by his T-shirt and kissed him right there in the doorway.

Caught by surprise, it took him a moment to find himself. Coming to his senses, he put one gentle hand around the back of her neck, slid the other around her waist, and pulled her close.

"Call me," she whispered.

"I will," Jesse said with a dopey smile. And just like that, Emi left for the second time that morning, grinning ear to ear. A second or two after she rounded the corner and was out of sight, she heard him give an audible "Yes!"

The crickets harmonized with the cicadas, throwing their song over a deep purple tree line. A lone streetlamp shone dimly on an old chain-link fence. The lot was deserted, and it was easy enough to forget that the inky park was surrounded by a busy city.

Emi and Fae giggled as their flip-flops crunched through the gravel, half-drunk beer bottles in hand. They walked in shadows toward the streetlight until a figure jumped out from behind them.

"God damn it, Matt! You're such a dick," Fae snapped.

"What gave me away?"

"I smelled your body spray all the way from the bar. That shit better not poison the water," she grumbled. "The last thing I want is to end up smelling like a thirteen-year-old boy."

"Don't lie. You know you like it," Matt teased.

He hooked his arm around her head and muscled Fae into a loose noogie. Emi's stomach leaped as she saw a familiar pair of white Nikes step into the circle of light.

"Hey guys," Jesse said with a grin. He opened his arms wide and came at Emi for a hug, squeezing her tightly. She was grateful for the dark as she felt herself turn red.

"Hey," was all she could say, her mind going completely blank. They looked at each other, smiling for a long second or two, almost close enough to kiss.

Emi remembered herself, and the girls led the way deeper into the park. Matt trailed a few steps behind, toting a case of Miller Lite and nervously eyeing the eight-foot fence. The bottles clinked with each step.

"Are you sure we're cool here?" he asked, trying to sound casual.

"Oh, yeah. We've been coming for years," Emi answered. "The cop cars can't see this far up the hill, so as long as we're quiet, we'll be fine."

Electricity shot through Emi as Jesse took her hand in his.

Fae instructed Matt to leave the case of beer outside the metal gate, which was roped and locked tightly to the other side of the fence, leaving an opening that was far too small for any person to squeeze through.

But the girls had figured out, over many nights of trial and error, that although none of them could sneak through themselves, they could certainly slide in a beer-laden hand.

As she had done a dozen times, Fae scaled the fence and hopped gracefully down to the other side, disappearing into the night.

"Need a hand?" Jesse asked chivalrously, but Emi laughed him off. She knew exactly what she was doing.

"Do I look like this is my first time? I invited you here, remember?"

Emi climbed the fence with quiet precision and easily dismounted behind the chain-link. She smiled at his wide-eyed expression, turned around, and pulled her T-shirt up and over her head, stripping down to just a thong and allowing the moonlight to bounce off her curves.

Jesse and Matt didn't hesitate any longer. They bumbled over the fence, clumsy and unpracticed.

Stifled conversation swirled with the thick smell of chlorine in the summer air. Darkness swallowed movement and shape, but the cloudy moon lit the surface of the water just enough to illuminate their faces.

Fae and Matt resumed their banter, relentlessly goading each other. But Emi found herself drifting deeper and deeper into the water with Jesse, farther and farther away from their friends.

"I was hoping you'd call me," she said coyly. She glided towards him, her naked body cutting through the warm water.

"How could I not?" Jesse reached out and hooked her waist to pull her into him. Her bare breasts rested gently on his warm chest, and goosebumps flooded her wet skin. They wrapped their arms and beers around each other, their friends a world away, laughing and splashing out of sight.

His lips found hers tenderly, though Emi quickly turned up the heat. Her head spun until she couldn't tell where she ended, and he began. Jesse threaded his fingers through Emi's wet hair, and her body tickled as he walked a hand down her spine, resting on the small of her back. She laid her arms over his damp, bulky shoulders, one hand on the scruff of his neck, the short-buzzed hairs prickling her fingers.

"It's awfully quiet over there," Fae teased from somewhere in the darkness. Emi giggled with embarrassment, letting her hands slide down Jesse's pectoral muscles.

She was safe in his arms, and she fit between them like a puzzle piece. It was as if they were made for her, like she belonged there.

"I like you," Jesse whispered. "A lot."

"I like you, too."

They sat on his bed, resting their backs on the headboard, a small bowl of snacks between them. Emi doubled over laughing at Will Ferrell, who had just shot himself with a horse tranquilizer on the fuzzy TV screen in front of them, propped up by old economy textbooks.

"You might be the most beautiful girl in the world," Jesse marveled, stars in his eyes while he watched her half choke on potato chips and gasp for air.

"Might be?" Emi croaked out.

"You are absolutely, without a doubt, the most beautiful girl in the world." She caught her breath, and he kissed her passionately. She climbed on his lap, sending the bowl of chips crashing to the ground.

The indigo sky flowed like Picasso's brushstrokes above as they laughed about something neither would remember later. Emi felt like she and Jesse were the last two people on Earth as they lay on a grassy knoll on the Schenley Park golf course, tripping off a handful of shrooms and peering into the heavens. The hill offered a million-dollar view of the city, and the lights from downtown sparkled just for them.

"I think I see Orion's Belt," Emi said excitedly, pointing at the constellation.

"I think you're right."

"Everything's all swirly, like a painting. Doesn't everything look swirly to you?"

"Yeah, kinda. Oh look, there's the Big Dipper."

But instead of following his pointed finger, Emi rolled over to watch Jesse.

"Your eyes are so shiny in the dark, just like the stars," she said.

"You're my star."

Emi giggled at his corniness and fell silent as they admired each other in the blue glow that surrounded them.

"I love you," Jesse confided. "I've always loved you. Like, since the minute we met. And sometimes I think, maybe, I've loved you forever."

"I love you, too."

The old row house basement was dark and crowded. Christmas lights were strung up around the walls, and music thumped. Emi walked purposefully around the two-story beer bong that poured from a hole in the kitchen floor above without giving it a second glance.

She came to a halt in front of a group of guys and boldly snatched a bottle of tequila from one of them, who was just raising it up for a swig, and guzzled it without asking.

"Hi, I'm Emi," she announced after wiping her mouth and shooting her most dazzling grin. "And this is my gorgeous best friend, Fae," she said, handing the liquor in her direction. Fae gave Emi a cosigning nose scrunch and smiled.

"Uh, I'm Sean," the boy closest to Emi stammered.

"Hi, Sean," Emi said, playing up her best coquettish giggle and eyelash-bat. They quickly fell into an animated banter, but after another round of frothy beers and bottle shots, Fae poked Emi hard in the ribs.

"What?"

"Em, he's coming," she hissed.

They watched on pins and needles, Emi's trap set, as Jesse's head bobbed over the mass of people. He stopped abruptly in front of her and after sizing up the situation, Jesse tried to pull Emi in for a hug, but she recoiled.

"What are you doing here? I thought we were meeting up later," he said. Emi didn't answer but took a long sip from her cup. "Who are these guys?"

"My new friends," she said flippantly. Though her bravado was blazing, she still couldn't look him in the eye. "Why don't you invite over your new friend? I'm sure you're dying to introduce us."

Emi nodded at the redhead across the way that Jesse had been talking to.

"That girl is Matt's cousin," he fired back. "Remember, I told you she was visiting. In fact, we were just talking about you."

"Oh, yeah? When she was stroking your arm?"

"Jesus, Emi. I was just being nice."

"Then why did Lydia text me that you were flirting with girls?"

"What? I'm sorry Lydia got the wrong impression, but I wasn't flirting. Now, let's go," he said. The circle of spectators waited with bated breath to see how this power struggle would end.

She sneered, taking a stand. "I'm talking to my new friend, Scott."

"It's Sean," the boy corrected.

"Fine. If that's how you want it. Good luck, Steve, you're going to need it," he said, and snatched Emi's drink out of her hand before turning away.

As Jesse stomped off, he threw back the contents of her cup and chucked it angrily at the cinderblock wall. On the outside, Emi snickered at his childish reaction. On the inside, she had to work hard to push aside her immediate regret.

He started it, she reminded herself. Disdain renewed, she turned her back on her boyfriend as his feet pounded up the old wooden stairs.

"Come on, Emi. We should go," Fae said. Even though her icy shell was melting fast, Emi didn't budge; she had dug herself in so far that she didn't know how to get out. But to her rescue, her best friend seemed to have understood her unspoken dilemma. Fae cleared her throat and shoved the tequila back at one of the boys. "Alright, kids. This has been fun, but we're out."

"I don't think Emi wants to leave," said Sean.

"Seth, is it? My friend, Emi here, is not going home with you. She won't be giving you her number. All she cares about is making her boyfriend jealous, which she's clearly accomplished. So, thanks for the liquor, but you can put it back in your fucking pants, buddy."

Impressed by her brash honesty, the boys—apart from Sean—broke out in a whooping round of applause. Fae stopped only to give her best royal bow, then pulled Emi to leave, arm in arm.

The minute she and Fae stepped through the front door and back outside, Jesse was there waiting on the sidewalk.

"What the fuck, Emi?" he demanded. Relief lifted her when she realized he was still there, but shame settled in quickly behind it with the look on his face.

"That was fucked up." He winced. "I would never act like that in front of you."

"Sure, you only act shady behind my back, right? Were you waiting out here just to fight with me?"

"I've never been shady with you, like, ever. I don't even look at other girls like that anymore. You're the only one, Emi." Jesse gave a cynical laugh. "You know, I was telling Matt's cousin how much I love you and how I was going to ask you to move with me to Ithaca. And then there you were—three feet away, taking shots with random frat boys? I know I'm jealous, too, but damn."

A switch flipped; all the anger in Emi halted. "You were going to ask me to move with you?"

"Yeah. I mean," Jesse said, his energy downshifting with Emi's. "I *am* going to ask you to move with me." He took a step closer. "I don't want to go without you."

Jesse

The apartment was small but sweet, with its ornate crown molding and arched gables. Snow-covered maple branches glistened in the third-floor windows. A cat slept lazily on the couch, and a small Christmas tree twinkled in the corner.

The peace erupted when the door slammed open, and two very cold, wet bundles spilled into the living room, almost on top of one another.

"Oh my God, turn the fire on!" Emi said through chattering teeth as she tore off her hat and scarf and dropped her coat and snow pants right where she stood. Jesse flipped the switch, and fire popped in the hearth. He pulled off all his wet clothes, hanging his and hers on the secondhand coat tree by the door.

"I got you good," he laughed.

"Oh, please. I nailed you with that last one."

"I don't think I've ever had a snowball fight with a girl before. Except my sister, but she doesn't count."

"A good thing, too, because I just kicked your ass. Honestly, you should be a little embarrassed."

"I love you," Jesse said, and pulled her close.

"I love you, too," Emi said. Her eyes danced in the firelight.

"I really love you."

"Well. I don't love you that much," Emi joked. "I'm going to put my comfies on."

She turned and headed down the hall, the wooden floor planks creaking with each step.

When she slipped out of sight, he snuck over to the red velvet stockings on the mantle. Jesse stuck his hand in deep and fished out a small ring box. Turning away from the bedroom door, he opened it to admire his grandma's small diamond ring glistening in the firelight.

He had been waiting all day for this moment. Actually, Jesse had been biding his time for two years, ever since they moved in together, and maybe even his whole life. But between his anxiety of making the moment special, his anticipation of what she might say, and how either way after tonight his life would irrevocably change, he couldn't contain himself much longer.

Quickly, he shut the box and put it carefully back in the stocking, just in time for Emi to return in her flannel penguin pajamas. She opened a drawer in the console table and started flipping through take-out menus.

"What do you feel like ordering?" she asked, absorbed by options. "Thai again?"

Emi bit the inside of her cheek in contemplation of dinner, and in that instant, Jesse knew he couldn't wait a second longer.

"I think Santa might have left you a Christmas Eve present in your stocking," he said. Jesse walked over to her and took her by the hand, leading her back to the fireplace.

The sun was setting over the Tyrrhenian Sea, blurring the watercolor sky the same hues as the small orange and pink houses that climbed the cliffs of the Amalfi Coast. Twilight set in as the fireflies danced over a meandering stone pathway leading to the edge of a magnificent mountain, high above the water, which crashed on the Faraglioni rocks below. Jesse waited under a rustic oak arbor, a light gray linen suit accentuating his dark eyes.

Jenna stood smiling at his side. Their mother sat front and center, in a polished antique chair, flanked by family and friends on either side of the stone aisle. A single violinist began to play as Fae and Rose made their way opposite him, both beaming in shades of muted pink.

And then, Emi. Jesse gasped. Ivory silk slid gracefully over her legs and trailed behind her as she floated toward the mountain's edge, under the luminary-lit branches of the olive trees.

On that one night, all was right in the Universe, and everything good was possible. A warm tear slid down Jesse's cheek and wet his lips as the stars shone upon them.

She reached him just as the sun slipped silently under the horizon. Jesse took Emi's delicate hands in his and promised to adore her for all eternity.

CHAPTER NINETEEN

Emi

Emi dug deep in her backpack as they stepped onto a dusty trail under a lush Costa Rican jungle. Tropical birds of every color called from high up in the lush, green leaves, small monkeys rustled branches just out of sight, and little green lizards darted up thick tree trunks.

About halfway up the mountain, they stopped for a break at an overlook. Below them, the jungle was a vast green sea. The sun shone high and hot as they took out their water bottles and sat together on a large, warm rock.

"I'm happy," Emi said quietly. "Like, really happy."

"Me, too," Jesse said. She put her head on his shoulder as he kissed the top of her hair and slid an arm around her. They sat for some time, admiring the view in blissful silence, content with each other and the world.

Their tans were darker in the shade of the private beach hut, with the bright blue waters of the Balearic Sea in front and the island of Ibiza behind them. Jesse stretched out on his lounger and looked at Emi, who was hard at work beside him.

"What if," he posed mischievously, "you put that away for now?"

Emi's sun-streaked high ponytail bobbed from behind her computer.

"That would be great, but I have to get this article to my editor by tomorrow morning," she answered, half amused, half annoyed. "Just because you're done pushing everyone's money around for the day doesn't mean I am."

"I know, but you're so pretty, you're the sexiest thing I've ever seen, and you're driving me crazy."

Emi rolled her eyes as she let him wrap his bulky arms around her and playfully tug at the bow that held her bikini top on.

"You're not going to leave me alone, are you?" She sighed, hitting save.

"Not unless you really want me to," he said in between light kisses up the curve of her neck.

Emi smiled coyly as she clapped her laptop shut. "Well, you'd better close the curtain then."

"Or we could leave it open and give these Spaniards a show." Jesse winked.

"Where are you now?" Fae asked.

Emi stood on the glass-paneled balcony of their hotel suite, wrapped in a spa robe, pinning the phone between her shoulder and her ear. A turquoise-blue ocean lapped peacefully against the beach as the sun broke over the white sand.

"Thailand. We will be here for five days and then to India to see the Taj Mahal."

"Damn, girl, I can't keep up. It's like, 'Where in the World is Emi Amato?'" Fae chortled. "But seriously, I'm so jealous. Was Bali just a dream? Your pictures are to die for. And you have the nerve to be all tan and sexy," Fae gushed, "while I'm over here pasty, with an extra twenty pounds of baby weight, secreting milk out of my boobs like a fucking cow. Plus, it's been raining for days, literally."

"Well, that's Pennsylvania for you. But it's not all sex and beaches here. The bugs are terrifying. I saw some kind of a beetle in my hotel room yesterday and thought for sure that was it—that was how I was going to die. It was the size of my hand. Swear."

"Ew! I take it back. Philly is just fine."

"I want to hear about you. How's my godbaby? Did you get the clothes I sent her?"

"Zoe's finally sleeping through the night. Which, by the way, is me bullshitting you. When I say 'through the night,' what I really mean is she's getting four hours at most."

"Jesus. I thought babies slept all the time?"

"Lies, Emi. It's all gaslighting and lies. Oh, and yes, I got the clothes. They are adorable. Thank God I had a girl."

"Ugh, I miss her. But what else is new? Did you guys close on the house yet? I feel like I've been gone for so long."

"The closing is next week, and we are insane. Never buy a house with a man, Em. The bickering. Oh my God, I can't. One hour of HGTV and Tyler thinks he's their next big house-flipper. It's truly more than one can bear."

"Oh, I'm sure," Emi snickered, watching a couple of dolphins cresting the water in the distance. "I can't believe you guys are on your second house already."

"Yeah, we're real adults or some shit. But for the record, I'm gonna need you to come home soon." Fae laughed. "I got married and had a baby, and you left me here to deal with these crazy-ass people on my own."

"We'll be home soon, the beginning of November," Emi reassured her.

"Wait . . . I thought we were meeting up in Pittsburgh for the Eagles game. I was really looking forward to it."

Emi held her breath, but her hesitation gave her away.

"Shit. I'm sorry, Fae. I guess I figured you wouldn't be up for it since you just had Zoe. I should have asked."

"Well, yeah, you should have. And you figured wrong. Just because I pushed out a kid doesn't mean I'm not still me, Em."

The wind rushed out of her, and Emi felt her heart twist.

"You're right, Fae. I just meant I thought you would be too tired. And Jesse really wanted to go to India, and it was the only time we could squeeze it in. Please forgive me. I promise I'll make it up to you. I'll come to Philly for a few days, and we can stay at the Four Seasons and get massages and facials, my treat."

She could feel Fae's disappointment through the phone. "Honestly, I love all the gifts and everything, but I really just

need you. Maybe now more than ever."

"I totally get it. I'm coming home soon, Fae. Cross my heart."

"Okay, well, you'd better be on my doorstep with an apology and a bottle of wine," Fae tried to joke, but she sounded resigned. "Jesse has to start sharing you. I feel like I hardly see you anymore."

Fae's last statement hit Emi's ego like a red-hot bullet. It was true she and Jesse were enjoying their adventures, but Fae had been the one to move across the state. She pushed her feelings of guilt and unfairness down.

"I promise we will spend more time together when I get home," she swore. "And I promise: I'll never miss our football games ever again."

Emi stared down at the cart full of bright fruit, salivating over a pile of mangos. The patchwork quilts, strung above her for shade, cast their purples, blues, and reds across her hands, and stretched all the way down the hill to the canal, where the street market ended, and the water market began. The noise barraged her, from bicycle bells to voices bargaining in languages she didn't speak. Glorious aromas wafted from large metal bowls of cooked rice, noodles, and soup, clashing with the smells of dried meat, fresh fish, and thick prawns that looked more like fat fingers.

Pretending to inspect a pair of handmade earrings, Emi posed a question as nonchalantly as possible.

"What do you think? Is it time?" she asked, afraid to look at Jesse.

"Time for what, lunch?"

"No. To like, you know, settle down. Maybe buy a house and start a family?" She held her breath as he took it in. Jesse didn't turn to look at her, and Emi wondered if he was hiding his face on purpose.

After a few moments that seemed like a lifetime, he spoke. "I don't know. Are you ready for all that?"

"Well, all my other friends have babies. And we're in our thirties now. I love our life, but—"

"I love our life, too. I just . . . I'm just not sure." Jesse stopped in the middle of the crowded street as if unable to think and walk at the same time. "Everything would change. I just don't know if I'm ready to share you yet. And we wouldn't be able to travel anymore."

"I think we still could, but our own home would also give us some stability. You know, it might be nice to plant our roots somewhere."

"Emi, I don't think you realize how much responsibility that is. A house means maintenance. If we're gone too long, and the heat's off, pipes could burst." Jesse was spiraling. "You need a landscaper and repair guy. There are birds in the attic and mice in the garage. The garbage disposal backs up, and then you have to paint the siding, stain the fence every few years, and power-wash the driveway. We couldn't just pick up and leave whenever we want anymore." He shook his head. "I took care of my mom's house for years. I don't want to do it again, at least not for a while."

"Fine, whatever. We don't need a house right now. But I still want a baby," Emi said, standing her ground. Jesse just looked at her blankly.

"Rose and I grew up traveling. And it made me who I am today," she pressed. "People travel with children all the time. Every flight we take, everywhere we go, people bring babies and little kids."

"Yeah, and it looks so stressful," he quipped. Her face flushed, and hot tears of betrayal stung her eyes.

"You've always said you wanted to have a family. You know how important that is to me."

"I do want a family. But maybe in a couple of years. I was thinking more like when we were thirty-five."

Their argument was blocking the flow of foot traffic, sending people scurrying around them. Jesse didn't seem to notice, and Emi was too swept up in her feelings to care.

"This isn't the first time we've talked about this," she said. "Your goalposts keep moving. How can I trust that you will ever be ready? It feels like you don't ever want a baby, and you're just placating me."

"I'm sorry I didn't give you a specific age before, but I guess I figured we were on the same page. I'm not placating you, Emi. It's fucked up that you would accuse me of that."

"Fine. I'll wait until we're thirty-five, but not any longer."

"What does that mean? You're going to leave me at thirty-five and one day if we don't have a baby by then?"

"No," Emi said. "Of course not."

Taking a deep breath to steady her nerves, she met his eyes, but instead of stubbornness, she found sadness. He was hurt, too.

"I promise we will have a family, but it will be on our time," Jesse pledged. "Not Fae's or anybody else's."

"Rosie, what's wrong?" Emi asked.

She set her wine glass down in Jenna's nineties, oak and blue laminate kitchen, watching Rose scowl. Bing Crosby crooned from the living room as their joined family gathered around a fat Christmas tree, wrinkling wrapping paper and waiting for turkey dinner. But in the kitchen, something felt off.

Rose grabbed the warmed dinner rolls out of the oven in a huff, an icy contrast to the merriment surrounding them. Awkward childhood photos of Jenna and Jesse's toothless grins beamed at them from the walls, as if they were snickering at the sisters' in their matching red buffalo plaid pj's.

"I just thought that when you guys bought a house, it would be closer to home. You know, where your family is."

Emi cleared her throat, a bit taken aback by Rose's resentment. "I never said that."

"Don't you want to be near us? I'm not even going to know your babies."

"What babies? Who even knows when babies will happen? And besides, we like exploring new places, Rosie. I've always wanted adventure."

"You mean Jesse wants adventure," she said with an eye roll.

"That's not fair."

"You've been saying for years that you want to settle down. But you guys are gone so much, it's like he's running away from something. And you just follow him anywhere," Rose sniped. "You used to be so independent. You used to have agency. You were the most self-reliant person I knew. I always admired that about you. But now your entire life revolves around a man."

Emi's eyes stung as if she had just been slapped in the face.

"Lower your voice, please. His whole fucking family is in the next room."

"Girls, could you bring the potatoes?" Jenna called from the dining room, as if on cue.

Emi moved to scoop the mashed potatoes out of a large pot on the stove and into a serving bowl. But Rose pushed her gruffly out of the way and took over.

"Give it to me," she snapped as she snatched the silver spoon.

"God, Rose. You are so fucking mean sometimes. What a shitty thing to say. I'm not ten anymore, and I still have agency. Treat me like an adult."

"Fine, Emi. I'm angry, and I'm hurt. And I think you've totally lost yourself in this guy."

"This guy?" Disdain washed over her. "This guy is my husband. We've been married for nine years. Have you secretly felt this way the whole time?"

"Kinda, yeah. And I'm not the only one."

Emi scoffed. "Well, marriage is something you know nothing about."

"I'm a fucking divorce attorney!"

"Maybe you know about divorce, but not marriage. At least, not a happy marriage."

Jesse rode into the kitchen on the heels of a small white dog that trotted happily toward the table. But he only made it two steps over the threshold before the strained silence sent him carefully backing out.

"I don't want to fight. I just . . . I miss you," Rose said.

"I miss you, too. But leave Jesse out of this. I'm a big girl, and I make my own decisions. And I certainly wouldn't live somewhere I didn't like. And he wouldn't want me to.

I know that we're gone a lot, but we want to see the world. We want to experience everything life has to offer. What's wrong with that?"

"Nothing is wrong with it. Unless you're missing out on the most important thing, which is family. I mean, it's nice you're here for the holidays, but Jenna and I barely see you, and now you're going to Japan for two months? How many places have you been this year?" Emi paused to count in her head, but Rose didn't wait. "What's the rush? Asia isn't falling into the sea."

"It's the best time for Jesse's schedule. Don't look at me like that, Rose. Marriage is about compromise. Sometimes, he wants to go somewhere, and sometimes, I do. I was the one who wanted a house, so we bought a house. And yeah, Jesse's always wanted to live in the mountains, but I also love Aspen. If I didn't, then we wouldn't have gone."

"You're all alone out there. All your friends and family are on the East Coast. I just feel like you've completely isolated yourself."

"Rosie, just because we live there now doesn't mean we will forever. Maybe we will if we want to, or maybe we'll have kids and move closer. We are so fortunate that we can afford to live wherever we want. I like my life the way it is."

"When was the last time you saw your real friends? Have you even talked to Fae lately? I saw her over Thanksgiving, and she said you two haven't spoken in months. She's not doing well. She almost cried when she saw me. Fae had a black eye, Em."

Emi's stomach dropped.

"I'm going to fucking kill him," she breathed. Beneath dizzying anger, guilt nested deep in her chest.

How could I not have known Fae needed me? Why didn't she call me? When was the last time we talked?

"You need to call her," Rose cut in as if she'd read her mind.

"Clearly. And I will."

"Emi, be honest with me. Are you really happy? Really?"

Emi put one hand on top of Rose's and looked her older sister squarely in the eye. "Yes, Rosie. I promise."

"It hurts me that I'm not part of your life anymore," Rose said, her eyes misting over. "I don't even feel like I'm on the periphery. I'm just an afterthought."

"Look, I know that I've let my relationships slide. But I want to change that. I want us to be close again. Like we used to be."

Rose wiped a tear away and put her arms around Emi, the large bowl of potatoes in between them.

"I told you, one day, you'd bring me here," Jesse said, eyes twinkling in the dark.

The Eiffel Tower sparkled behind them, a cool wind blowing through her hair over the Pont des Arts bridge. Jesse's arms were wrapped around her to keep the November chill at bay, but he let one slide off her back to dig into his wool coat.

He pulled something out of the pocket. It shone in the moonlight as he held it up to her eyes.

At first, Emi didn't know what she was looking at. He handed her the bicycle lock, and she lit up as she realized what it was. Something black and frayed was tied tightly around the hook.

"What is that?" she asked, needlessly. Her fingers traced the stretchy string, igniting her muscle memory.

"You know what it is," he said.

"Wait, is this . . ."

"Yeah. Something told me to go back for it the next day."

Emi's eyes flooded, and she couldn't help the fat tears that rolled down her face. He kissed her there in the dark, under the lamppost, on their bridge of locks.

She was meant to be here. Beyond the Eiffel Tower, under the lamp post, on Love Lock Bridge, with Jesse. The Universe and stars—her whole life—had led her to this magical moment in time. And she never wanted to leave.

"Well, where should we put it?" he asked.

The fence was so engulfed with locks that it was hard to find a spot, but she bolted the clasp around a small piece of empty chain-link and smiled.

"Make a wish," Jesse said, kissing the little silver key before throwing it into the river.

Emi closed her eyes.

I wish for us to be in love like this forever.

After watching the dark water ripple for a while, they walked away, holding hands. Emi's old hair tie, knotted tightly around their love lock, was left to dance in the Parisian wind.

Jesse

"What's wrong?" Jesse asked. But from the look on Emi's face, he knew it was serious.

She shut the bathroom door and stood in the bedroom, looking dazed and disconnected from her body. He didn't need her to answer him. He already knew.

"I'm bleeding," Emi said quietly. Jesse turned off the TV and got up.

"Well, you've had spotting before, right?" he asked hopefully. He walked her back to their bed, easing her down and propping her legs on a pillow, then sat next to her and gently laid a hand on her abdomen.

"It's different this time, Jesse," she said, gazing trance-like out the window. He barely registered the heavy raindrops that splattered noisily against the roof and shook the tall spruces outside their bedroom. Her chin quivered. "It's more than spotting."

Please, God, if you're there, please let my wife and this baby be okay. I promise I'll be the best husband and father. Please.

"Let's call the doctor," he said.

Jesse pulled his baseball hat down further over his face, pretending to shield himself from the bright sunlight, though he was really hiding his misty eyes from his little sister. Showing her anything but strength and dependability made him uncomfortable.

Jesse was always the shoulder to cry on for Jenna. It wasn't supposed to be the other way around.

"I'm so sorry, Jesse," Jenna said, pausing for his dog to sniff around a fat tree trunk. "It's just a really shitty situation. I'm happy I'm here to help."

"I'm happy you're here, too. She's doing better, but she hasn't been eating much. You'll see when she gets home. I'm just worried, I guess."

"Well, Stella here"—she bent down and fluffed the beagle's ears—"is helping just fine. I think a puppy was a great idea. Isn't that right, Stella?"

Stella gave out an excited yip, and they continued down the sidewalk and into Aspen's quaint downtown. Jesse swallowed the lump in his throat and built up the courage to broach the uncomfortable question he had brought Jenna all the way from Pittsburgh to ask.

"I know it was different circumstances, and it was years ago, but I was hoping you could talk to Emi about your own miscarriage," he said.

"I'm happy to talk to her, but she just needs rest and time. What did the doctor say?"

"They had to do an internal ultrasound because it was early on. It was big enough to see it on the monitor, but it hadn't grown at the rate it should have. And unlike last time, she was spotting but not bleeding enough. They had to do a D&C."

"Oh, Jess. That's terrible. How many weeks was she?"

"Eight. The doctor explained that it was supposed to be the size of a raspberry and had probably stopped developing some time before. But she said to give it a month or two, and then we can try again. I had no idea miscarriage was so common."

Jesse paused to watch Stella's clumsy trot, more grateful to his new puppy than he could say. She was the best medicine he'd ever purchased.

After that horrible doctor's appointment, Emi had spent a week lying on her side, catatonic on their bed. Until Jesse had tiptoed in one day with Stella in his arms, a bow around her pink collar, and slipped the little beagle beside her.

Emi had sat up, startled, and scooped Stella close. She cried as they nuzzled each other, allowing the dog to heal her broken heart.

"Anyway," he said, his throat tight with emotion he tried to hold down. "I know when you had your miscarriage, we were out of the country. And watching Emi go through it, I just wanted to tell you again how sorry I am that I wasn't here for you."

Jenna didn't say anything, but Jesse knew her silence meant something.

"Are you still upset with me about it?" he asked cautiously.

"No," Jenna sighed. "Let's get our coffees first." She nodded at the outside seating of a little café. Jesse left Jenna and Stella in their seats in the sun and went inside to fetch their drinks. He couldn't help but notice the frown on Jenna's face through the window and wondered if there was something he didn't know.

She waited until he situated himself in his seat before she spoke. "I didn't have a miscarriage, Jesse," Jenna said, her stare boring into Stella, curled in her lap. Jesse was confused.

"What do you mean?"

She took a deep breath and looked up. "I had an abortion."

Jesse sat, befuddled, like he was trying to find the words in a different language.

"Well, say something," Jenna said. "I mean, it's fine if you hate me or think I'm a murderer or going to hell. I just need some kind of a response."

"Okay," Jesse said slowly. He was so ashamed of himself.

How could I not know such a big thing about my sister, the little girl it was my mission to look out for? How could I have let her go through that alone?

"I don't think you're any of those things, Jen. I could never." He choked on emotion. "I'm so sorry. I'm so sorry I wasn't there for you. You must have been so scared."

"Well, yeah, I was. But it's okay now. I just couldn't raise a child by myself," Jenna said, tears of guilt welling in her eyes. "I know we were brought up to—"

Jesse wrapped his arms around her, cutting her off. "I don't care how we were brought up."

"I just couldn't do it on my own. And we all know my ex would have been long gone before any responsibility came his way," she said.

"Why didn't you ask me for help? We would have helped you and supported you either way."

"I know." She wiped tears from her face. "But you spent half your life taking care of me and Mom. You have a wife who needs you now. You don't need to worry about us anymore, and especially a child that isn't yours."

"Why didn't you at least tell me?" Jesse implored. "We could have at least been with you. What if something had gone wrong?"

"You and Emi were traipsing around the world, and I didn't want you to come back just for me."

Jesse frowned. His worst fear was letting his family down, and he had. Big time.

"Jesse, you're a wonderful big brother," Jenna swore, and she smiled sadly, patting his hand. "I just wasn't meant to be a mom."

Emi

Emi's sweaty fingers threaded through Jesse's and squeezed tighter and tighter as the plane lurched sixty thousand feet over the Atlantic Ocean.

Flight attendants strapped themselves into their safety harnesses. The cabinet doors were banging open and closed above them.

"It's okay, Em. I've got you," Jesse said steadily in her ear. "We're okay, promise."

"Why didn't you tell me?" Emi begged. "I would have come for you, you know that. Fae, I would have done anything to be there for you."

Fae set the candle she had been huffing back on its shelf and waited for the other group of boutique shoppers to pass them by before she answered.

"I don't know. I'm ashamed and embarrassed," she said quietly, hanging her head.

"What? Nobody deserves to be abused by their husband. Ever."

"I'm ashamed that I let myself get here. And that I stayed for so long. I put the girls in danger by staying, too. I'm a terrible mother. How could I have done that to them?" She wiped tears quickly from her eyes before anyone else could see.

"No, don't say that. You're a great mom."

Fae cleared the hurt from her voice.

"But also, though, Emi. You're like, not really in my life anymore."

Ice shot through Emi's veins.

"I . . ." she stammered, trying to find some kind of defense. "You're right. I'm sorry."

"Like, the girls don't even ask about you anymore. Haven't you noticed I pretty much stopped calling?"

She hadn't.

"Yes," Emi lied. "I guess I just . . . I'm sorry. I've been so caught up in my work and the fertility stuff, traveling, and maybe Jesse, too. I've just sort of let things get away from me."

She took Fae's hand. "But I'd like to change that if you'll let me. You're my sister, Fae. Forever."

Fae smiled and sandwiched Emi's hand in kind. "Yeah, I would like that, too."

Emi stepped out from the thick steam of the cobblestone shower. She towel-dried her hair in the mirror, then turned to Jesse through the open door leading into the bedroom. He was snug under a big white down comforter, glasses on and book in hand. Beyond him twinkled the lights of the tiny resort town of Zermatt, tucked into the side of the Swiss Alps. His eyes found hers as marshmallow snowflakes drifted down through the night.

The tension in his jaw dissipated, for which she was grateful. The friction between them had subsided since their argument over dinner, like the settling of a stormy sea.

There was nothing worse than when he was angry with her.

Emi sensed a dissension approaching. She could feel it building a mile away. It was the day before her fortieth birthday, and her emotions ran raw since she opened her eyes that morning. Her foul attitude persisted, and she spent the day in a dark mood.

A month ago, Emi was excited about starting a new decade. She had a sexy, kind, adoring husband. They had money and a beautiful home. They explored the world together and enjoyed the luxury most people coveted. She had her dream job, after years of freelance bullshit, as a successful novelist. Not to mention, she felt more radiant and confident in her skin than ever. Life was easy and sweet, with only one void left unfilled, though it was a big one. Maybe the biggest. She didn't have a baby.

Emi and Jesse agreed to try until she turned forty. And here it was, smacking her in the face. They had talked seriously about adopting or surrogacy but decided against it. Thousands of dollars were spent on in vitro to no avail. Late-night prayers, hormone injections, fertility tests, doctor's appointments, holistic therapies, bartering with God, and acupuncture had all failed. Jesse flew her to Bhutan to pray at the fertility temple, bought her special beaded bracelets in Sri Lanka, and merlinoite and moonstone from a Reiki master in Japan.

Emi had been pregnant three times over the last five years. And each time, within a few weeks, she wasn't anymore.

The emotional turmoil, the toll on her body, and the stress on her husband and marriage all needed to come to an end. Emi knew her childhood dream had run its course. It was time to accept that life had a different plan for them.

Emi thought she had come to peace with it. She really had. She told herself that a life of forever adventure with Jesse was enough.

But in the deep night, she had a beautiful dream of holding a smushy pink bundle of a newborn baby. When Emi woke up, she could still feel the weight of her tiny daughter cooing in her arms as she heard herself whisper,

"*Oh, it's you. I'm so happy to see you again.*"

And all over again, Emi's heart was crushed into a thousand pieces, bleeding her out, knowing her most cherished wish would slip away, never to materialize into reality in the morning light.

All day, Emi despaired. She held back tears on the ski course, at the hot chocolate station, and at the five-star Michelin restaurant. Her despondency in the Alps, one of the most breathtaking places on Earth, was just more salt in her open, festering wound.

Sometimes it annoyed her that Jesse knew her so well. He could see the pain in her eyes, how she cocked her head to one side when she choked back tears, and her trite, fake little smile. And it pissed her off that she couldn't hide from him.

It was her birthday, for fuck's sake, and she just wanted to wallow without the extra weight of guilt for ruining his vacation, too.

"Emi, I can't take it anymore," he'd said once the waiter left their crème brûlée and macaroons on the table. "We are in the best ski resort on the planet, and I'm watching you cloud it for yourself. You know I would have loved to have been a father, and I have done everything I possibly can to make that happen for us."

She glared into her cappuccino. "I can think of one thing you didn't do. We could have started trying sooner."

"The doctor said we would have had the same issue. More time wouldn't have helped."

"More time would have meant more opportunity. Who's to say if it would have helped?"

Emi knew she wasn't being fair. But nothing about the situation was fair, and she couldn't stop her spite.

"And I love that you have the privilege to say you 'can't take it anymore.' I don't have the liberty to disassociate"—she'd hissed out the word—"and pretend like I'm fine."

"Why not?"

Emi could feel her eyes flash red-hot.

"Because I'm the woman, and it's my fucking body betraying us, so it's all my fault. I'm the one who got turned into a desperate Dr. Jekyll and Mr. Hyde every month. I rode the pendulum of sobbing on the floor, having my body taken over with all-encompassing anger or severe biological depression for the last five years. I'd like to see you inject yourself with hormones for egg harvesting and watch you put your feet in the stirrups to have inanimate objects jammed up your organs for IVF."

"Okay, so does that mean that my experience is completely invalid? It wasn't exactly a fucking vacation watching the love of my life tortured for years, helpless and incapable."

They called a draw, paid the bill, and left with dessert untouched. Emi and Jesse shuffled through the soft snow, walking slowly to avoid slipping on the town's half-shoveled sidewalks.

"Don't you know how sad I am that I couldn't do anything to help? It broke my heart to watch you go through all of that," he'd said, "and each time I picked you up and carried you to bed, I waited quietly for you to come back to me. Sometimes I wasn't as patient, and sometimes I yelled back at you. But my heart broke, just like yours, every time," he said, pausing his anger long enough to hold her hand through thick gloves and ensure she didn't fall.

Frozen tears streaked her face as they rounded the street, heading toward the warmth of their cabin. "Jesse, I'm sorry. I know I'm being an unfair bitch. You've always been there for me. For us." She sniffled. "I know you're devastated, too. I'm just so sad."

He nodded curtly in acknowledgment. They ducked into the foyer to unbundle, then walked up the glass staircase toward the primary suite.

"I get it. Your birthday marks the end," Jesse said as he hung his head. "I'm sorry I couldn't give you a baby." He looked at her imploringly. "But I need you, Emi. I know you're still in there. I know you're still you."

"I am. Let me take a shower, and I'll come back."

As Emi climbed into the steam shower and let herself cry, she made up her mind that when she came out, she would let go of the baby that never was. The weight of her grief and pain had been an anchor, threatening to pull them under. It was too much to carry anymore.

It was time to release what wasn't to be, find meaning in the life she had, and stop pining for a reality that wasn't meant for her.

When Emi walked out of the bathroom—hair damp from the towel-dry, big puffy snowflakes dancing in the air beyond the large glass windows—she was smiling. Life had not always been easy, especially lately, but they loved each other endlessly. That never faltered.

As she dropped her towel, Emi snatched the book from his hands and tossed it aside.

In the morning, the sun rose over the glistening Swiss mountaintop. Emi stretched and sighed under the covers as she rubbed her eyes in the brilliance of a new day. Jesse traced the curve of her body as snow drifted gently by their window.

"There you are," he said, running a forefinger down her nose. She squinted into the bright light, and Jesse came into focus. "I've been waiting for you to wake up. My beautiful birthday girl."

CHAPTER TWENTY

They stepped into the long hallway, hand in hand. White light pulsed around the thin wooden door as Jesse closed it carefully behind them. The intense moments Emi had just experienced overwhelmed her body, and bewilderment stifled every thought.

After a quiet moment, they turned to each other. Emi found Jesse's eyes filled with all the sentiment and passion of their life together. They made their way back to the foyer in silence, where the large glass windowpanes revealed the other side of the street. Jenna and Rosie were waiting in the same spot as if she and Jesse had just left them moments before.

"How'd it go?" Rosie asked as soon as they stepped outside.

"Okay," Emi said. She looked up at Jesse and smiled. "I mean, it was amazing."

"It was," Jesse said as he slid an arm around her waist. His hands were big and warm, and Emi remembered how safe and protected she felt in their life together.

"Before you make your final decision, let's walk," Rosie said. She turned and led them down the street to the little park they had cut through on the way to the apartment.

"Hey, Rosie?" Emi called. Rosie slowed down to let her catch up. "Where are we, exactly? I mean, this isn't my memory anymore, right?"

"Right." She nodded toward the end of the street. "Now we are in the In-between."

"In-between what?" Jesse interjected.

"Everything," Rosie laughed. "The In-between is a place of its own."

"How many different 'places' are there?"

"An unlimited amount. New places are created and extinguished as needed." She gestured for them to pass through the ivy-covered gate that swung open into the park. "Think of it as a classroom in an infinite school. And this room is reserved just for you two."

As Emi stepped through the gateway, a chill tickled up her spine. The park on the corner of the city block melted away, and they were suddenly in a meadow surrounded by thick woods. The ivy-covered gate was still behind her, out of place, alone at the edge of an autumn forest.

Tall pines canopied them, and beyond the woods, distant oaks and maples threw a celebration of red and yellow. A breeze swooshed the tops of the trees and lifted a few stray leaves to dance in the wind. The air was crisp, and the sun beamed down happily from the cornflower sky.

Four curved benches sat patiently in a circle surrounding a stone fountain in the middle of the clearing. They walked single file through tall grass and wildflowers to take their seats, Emi and Jesse on one bench, Jenna and Rosie on another.

"I know this place," Emi said with certainty.

Jesse took in his surroundings and cocked a brow. "I think I do, too."

"Yes," Jenna said. "This is your room in the In-between."

And all of Emi's dreams came rushing back. "The psychic said we were meeting up while we were sleeping," she whispered, almost to herself, assembling the puzzle pieces. She turned to Jesse. "This is where we were. We were here."

Visions of the love they shared there bombarded her. She saw Jesse grin at her in their white bed under the trees and laugh as the bluebirds darted back and forth. Then came their argument when he said he couldn't meet her in the diner, and the empty field from her anger and despair when he didn't show.

"So, Fae's been right all along," Emi said with a smile, her pride swelling. "My dreams are prophetic. So, does that mean I'm really gifted, too?"

"Yes, you are. You just never understood it before." Rosie smiled, and Emi sat with this for a moment.

"What happens now?" Jesse asked.

"If the two of you decide to start a new timeline in a new dimension," Jenna answered, "it will spur off, just like you saw, from the moment Emi decided to return to your apartment instead of leaving that morning after you tried to kiss her."

"Do you remember what made you turn around?" Rosie asked Emi.

"It was the bird, right? It came back."

"That's right. The bluebird really is your guide. That's why you could hear her when she warned you against running away."

"Oh my God," Emi marveled. "So, she's been with me my whole life?"

"Yes. Sometimes you were meant to notice her, even interact with her. Sometimes not, but she's always been there to help you, and she always will be. If you decide you want to be with Jesse, she will be waiting for you on top of your car, just as you saw."

Jesse furrowed his brow. "Wait. So, do I have a guide, too?"

"Yes," Jenna assured him. "Everyone does. And more than one. You're never just out here in life all on your own. You're always surrounded by your pit crew of passed loved ones, spirit guides, and angels."

"What happens if we can't agree or if we both choose to stay in our current lives?" he asked.

"In both cases, you will wake up in your different beds the night before the football game. You both will go about your day as normal. But the Universe will add protections that act like the inflatable sides on a bowling lane. They will keep you on the straight and narrow, making sure you don't go off course . . . and making sure you do not see each other." Emi and Jesse shared a concerned look.

"Like, at all?" Emi asked. The idea hurt her heart.

"Nope, not at all. For instance, Jesse, you'll be held up in the stands, which will delay you by mere minutes, but long enough to ensure Emi leaves the beverage cart before you arrive."

A glimpse of the possibility floated before her eyes: A belligerent Patriots fan, screaming during a big play, accidentally knocked Jesse's phone out of his grasp, smashing it on the ground. Embarrassed, the man helped Jesse pick up all the little pieces from underneath the folding seats while professing how sorry he was.

"And Emi," Rosie continued, "you and Fae will be so excited for a weekend without kids. The night before the game, you'll drink too much. You'll be so hungover in the morning that you'll stick to your seat as much as possible, keeping you far away from Jesse.

And all the signs you have been seeing for months—the dreams and eerie feelings—will stop. Jesse, you will be left with the conclusion that you need to make some changes in your life. And Emi, this whole experience will elevate your energy and kick off your spiritual awakening. And you will both decide that, though there may be a part of you that still longs for what might have happened, it just wasn't meant to be. And you will move on enough to live happily without each other."

But now that she'd experienced their life together, Emi couldn't fathom the idea of not being with Jesse. And then Vi's face ran past her mind, then Jack's and Liam's. And then Josh. Sweet Josh.

How could I possibly live without my family?

The idea shook her to the core and tore her in two.

"Okay, so what if we do decide to start a new life? Nothing happens to Josh and my children, right? Explain this to me again, because I need to be certain they will still be happy, good, and just the way they are meant to be without anything changing for them. Because, Rose, you know I would never compromise their futures. For anything. Ever."

"I promise, Emi. Their timelines would continue untouched. Though your consciousness will be with Jesse, another piece of your soul will still be with your family, living out that lifetime with them. What you would be doing is simply choosing to divert your attention."

"Wait a second. If we can create a dimension where my kids were never conceived, then that means there are dimensions where I don't exist, right?"

"I know that's hard to comprehend, but yes."

"If Emi and I decide to go back and change things . . ." Jesse looked to Jenna, working it out for himself, too. "Does that mean Caleb was never born?"

"He'll only be in your original life," Jenna said. "Just like Emi's children. But you won't be conscious of him at all."

Jesse flinched, and his eyes went wide.

Emi broke the silence. "So, we would be giving up the most important relationships we have to be with our Primary Soulmate." She paused, looking for a workaround. "Can we make a pact to be together in our next life if we choose to stay where we are?"

"You could try, but nothing is guaranteed. The lessons you may or may not learn in this life directly impact your future incarnations. Karma is absolute. There's no getting around it."

"So, it could be all or nothing?" Jesse asked.

"It could be," Rosie answered.

A flock of birds flew overhead, and they could hear the bubbling of the fountain.

"Do you have any other questions?" Jenna asked. They shook their heads. "Then we will leave you here. Remember, when you've made up your mind, you don't need to do anything. You will simply wake up in whatever life you've chosen without any memory of this, and everything will seem as if it has always been."

Jenna hugged Jesse tenderly, and, in turn, Rosie squeezed Emi close.

"I love you, Em," Rosie said. "We are soulmates, too, you know. And I cherish our lives together."

"I think I've known it my whole life. I love you, too," Emi said, her fat, splashy tears watering her big sister's hair while they embraced. They wiped their cheeks, and Rosie took Emi by the shoulders to look into her eyes with a smile.

"Remember, there's no wrong decision. Neither option is better or selfish. This is not a test. Life is a journey that we get to create. Enjoy it."

Emi turned her head as the shifting clouds above caught her attention. When she looked back to the spot where Rosie had been standing, she wasn't surprised to find that she and Jesse were alone again.

Emi curled into him on the bench, and he draped his arm around her. She snuggled into his cozy green hoodie and breathed in the scent she knew so well. Together, they watched the water spill from the top of the fountain and into the large stone basin.

"This is why you smell like you do," Emi said.

"What do you mean?"

"You smell like an enchanted forest. You smell like here."

"So do you," Jesse said, bending down and picking one of the pink flowers that sprouted in tufts at their feet, tucking it into her hair. "I guess we've always known we belong together."

"Penny for your thoughts?"

"I think," Jesse said as he lifted her chin so he could look at her, "you have the most beautiful eyes I have ever seen. In all my lives. And I will know them anywhere."

"No, dummy." She blushed. "I meant, have you decided what you want to do about us?"

"Yeah, have you?"

Emi nodded. Before she could say another word, he put a finger up to her lips.

"What if we don't talk about it? I mean, I don't want to sway you. What you choose to do with your life should be your own decision. And we won't remember when we wake up, regardless. We will either be together or we won't. And if not, we won't know what we had together, anyway. Or, I mean, what we could have together."

Emi stared straight ahead. It broke her heart to know he was right. One way or another, she would forget a beautiful life—one with Josh and the kids or one with Jesse.

He sighed. "I'll either be loving you or getting over you the rest of my life."

Emi peered up into his dark eyes. No matter how much she tried to deny it, she had always known that Jesse was the strongest connection she ever felt. There was something cosmically unbreakable binding them together. No amount of space or time had weakened it, and she knew then it never would.

Emi breathed out. "You're right. Instead of going back and forth about it, let's just enjoy this time together, here, in this place that was made just for us."

With his fingers in her hair, he kissed her so sweetly, so passionately, with all the tenderness of a thousand lives lived together. Every joule of energy flowed seamlessly between their bodies, like reconnecting the ends of a cut wire, plugging them back into the Universe.

Emi saw herself sitting on a damp hotel bed, looking at herself in her hand mirror, somewhere in time, and her words from so long ago circled in her mind. "A supernova, worlds-colliding, stars-exploding, once-in-a-lifetime kind of love."

She rested her head on his brawny chest and sighed. "I love you. I always have."

"Watching the life we had together was incredible," Jesse mused. "I don't really have words for it. 'Love' doesn't even come close."

"I know."

Two bluebirds floated gracefully to a branch nearby. Emi and Jesse sat silently for some time as they watched them perch.

"Tell me about your life," Jesse said. "The one without me. I want to know everything."

Emi told him about her disappointment and despondence after things between them hadn't worked out, falling in love with Josh, their struggles, and accomplishments. She went on about becoming a mother to each of her kids, Rosie and Fae, her hopes and dreams, romance, and heartache.

Jesse spoke about his own dismay over their stifled love, Caleb and Jenna, his parents, and his career. He went into detail about his travels, the countries he'd been to, and the many girlfriends from whom he had learned so much.

They discovered how many times they'd circled each other before and after college. Sometimes missing each other by minutes and seconds, never quite intersecting until the baseball clinic.

Finally, they shared their experiences with the life they could have. They talked for a long time about their own romance and marriage, their travels and passion, and their sorrow and resentment at being unable to conceive. But more than anything, they confessed their deep, undeniable, and unshakable devotion and understanding for each other.

In a place where time mattered, the conversations would have taken days. But in their woods, love was the only quantifiable. Puffy white clouds drifted above them while leaves swayed like waves, and the day would go on for as long as they needed.

As the sun began to slide behind the trees, the bluebirds quieted, and evening slipped in. Emi's fingers were still wrapped up tightly in Jesse's hoodie, never wanting to let him go. But with each thump of his heart, they slowly evaporated into nothingness.

"I'll see you again soon, Emelie Amato. I promise," he whispered in her ear. "I'll love you forever."

As they disappeared, a new sensation materialized, washing over Emi's desperation and fear of losing Jesse. It was a feeling she had never known before. At first, she was freefalling, plummeting through what felt like empty air into nothingness. But then, as her trajectory began to slow, she realized she was falling, then floating, through something tangible.

CHAPTER TWENTY-ONE

She fell through a wide tunnel of color-changing vapor. Emi reached out curiously and put her hand into the rainbow mist, and her fingertips ran down long, thin strands of translucent, vibrating threads.

I'm falling through energy.

Fragments of color raced past her eyes, and what had been a loud, pulsating, whooshing sound—like a sonogram heartbeat—petered out to make bits of words and then conversations. As Emi's trajectory decelerated, her mind caught up with the scenes playing out in front of her.

A three-year-old Violet splashed happily in their small bathtub, spraying water on Josh while he and Emi laughed together.

A newborn baby—Jack—was placed in Josh's arms, wrapped snugly in a Pittsburgh Steelers Terrible Towel. He handed him off to Emi as she lay in the hospital bed, then kissed her on the head. She looked down at her boy with wonder, and little Jack blinked his small, turtlelike eyes up at her.

Josh beamed. "We have a son."

"Stop being such an asshole," she hissed at Josh on a street corner as they rambled home after a long night at the bar.

"What the hell are you even mad at me for?" Josh yelled back, incredulously and slurring.

Emi hiccupped. "I don't know!"

A golden retriever puppy went running past the Christmas tree in their small craftsman home, almost knocking it over. The tree wobbling, Josh chased the dog as Emi belly laughed on the couch, spilling her latte.

Emi held baby Liam's hands and slowly walked alongside him through their living room. As she gently let go, he teetered toward Josh.

"You can do it, Liam!" Violet and Jack cheered from the floor, ready to catch their little brother as he took his first steps.

Emi and Josh were twisted up, naked, in the sheets. He pushed a piece of hair behind her ear.

"I'll love you forever," he whispered.

The Easter egg hunt in Grandma's backyard was chaotic, with little kids rushing everywhere. Josh held Violet's pudgy hand while the children ravaged the bushes and flower beds.

"Over here!" Rose called, careful not to spill her sangria as she pointed out a blue egg behind a hydrangea bush.

She and Violet lay in bed in goopy face masks, a bowl of popcorn between them. They giggled as old reruns played on TV.

Emi, Fae, and Rose danced barefoot under the stars at her wedding reception, singing loudly and spinning like little girls.

During a sonogram appointment, Josh and Emi looked hard at the monitor, hoping to see some sign of life.

"I'm sorry," the doctor said quietly.

A moving truck pulled in front of a large, white-brick house with black shutters on a grassy knoll. Emi and little Jack sat under their new cherry tree, watching it begin to unload.

Violet peered up at her. "Is this our new home, Mamma?"

"Yes, baby," she said.

Emi and Josh were caught up in a delirious middle-of-the-night exchange.

"God damn it, we're out of sheets," Emi proclaimed through desperate tears. "He's thrown up on all of them. Josh, I need your help. I can't do this by myself."

"Just put some towels down," Josh moaned.

"Mamma!" Liam wailed as he ran into the hallway and then threw up all over the floor.

Emi and Fae stumbled drunkenly off the boardwalk and over the dune that looked out onto the wide beach. They laughed like teenage girls, hiked up their denim miniskirts, and plopped in the sand. They shared a large bottle of Bacardi and pointed out dolphins cresting as the sun rose over the Atlantic Ocean.

Behind the glass window of the NICU, Emi held Violet and sang quietly to her. She was determined not to cry as she carefully rocked her baby, trying not to disturb the tubes that stuck out of her little body, or the oxygen monitor around her tiny newborn toe.

"Shh, it's okay, Vi. Mommy's here. You're okay."

Emi lay in a bubble bath, her pregnant belly cresting from the water. Little Liam dragged a foot inside her womb and rippled not just her stomach but the water around it.

She sat on the cold metal bleachers, cheering on Jack at his baseball playoffs. *Just one hit*, she prayed. *Please, give him one hit . . .*

Emi cried with Fae, hugging her tightly as she felt tears soak her shoulder. They stood in the middle of Fae's living room, surrounded by packed boxes.

"You're not alone, Fae. You're never alone. You and the girls always have us. We're family."

Emi and Josh sat on the porch stairs, watching the fireflies light up in the dark as they passed a glass of wine under the stars.

Rose held Violet tightly on her lap and comforted her as she cried loudly at her fourth birthday party. Josh and Emi chased the cake-covered dog as pink frosting fell from her nose.

All three kids startled Emi and Josh as they jumped on their bed at five-thirty a.m. on Christmas morning, screaming,
    "Santa came! Santa came!"

Emi held Josh's hand in a church pew as he wept at a friend's untimely funeral.

Fireworks on the beach cracked green, red, and blue in the night sky. Josh held Emi tightly during the finale, a ring sparkling on her finger.
    "I'm the luckiest man alive," he said into her ear.

Emi tiptoed into the living room of the lake house and turned off the TV, trying not to disturb Rose and Jack, who had fallen asleep snuggling on the couch, surrounded by popcorn and candy bowls, as the moon shone on the water outside.

Josh and Emi lay on the floor of the animal hospital, bent over their first dog. They were sobbing, praying, and telling her they loved her and that she was the best dog anyone had ever had. Emi whispered in her soft, furry ear that it was okay to let go as Josh's tears dropped heavily, one after the other, into her yellow tufts.

"I hate you!" Violet screamed, red-faced and wild, at the top of the stairs. Emi's lip quivered as she held back tears.

Emi and her girlfriends laughed in a hot tub. The cabin lights warmed the windows, and the stars twinkled in the night sky.

Emi watched Liam cackle with delight as he and the dog took turns running through the sprinkler on the lawn.

Violet's pink-painted fingernails wrapped around Emi's hand, and she giggled as Josh gently pushed them in the hammock on their island.
 "I think I dreamt about this once," Emi said. Violet looked up at her with big amber eyes.

Jack's three-year-old thick black eyelashes swept over Emi's as they laughed and laughed at their tickly butterfly kisses and each other's joy.

Emi and Josh held hands as they jumped into the empty air and plunged toward the Mediterranean Sea. He squeezed her hand midflight, and she closed her eyes as her feet barreled toward the turquoise water below.

CHAPTER TWENTY-TWO

2022

"The girls are coming, too, right?" Emi asked into the otherwise silent car.

"That's the plan," Fae answered, her voice crackling through the speaker mounted over the driver's seat. "Do you need us to come early? Thanksgiving is a lot of work."

"Sure, that would be great. And, of course, Rosie will help."

"Cool. I'm dying to hear about your trip, though. Tell me."

"Oh my God, it was everything. Josh and I haven't traveled without the kids in years. We really needed it."

"It was so nice he surprised you like that."

"I know. He's really making an effort to be more attentive, especially now that the kids are a little older. And Miami was the best. We had all the sex and drinks and fun. I was thinking, Fae, I'm feeling good about this whole forty thing. I really feel like you and I are beginning to find ourselves again."

"I think so, too," Fae said.

"Oh, I'm here. I'll call you later."

Emi parked under a large tree. The crisp autumn air turned her nose and cheeks pink, and she was grateful for her quilted jacket and scarf. She smiled as she walked past fat pumpkins adorning the stoops of old townhouses. Yellow and red leaves hung above her like jewels on a chandelier, and she wondered if she had accidentally wandered onto a Hallmark movie set.

Emi stopped before a thin brick building and pushed through the antique door. Bells jingled, and a woman poked out from behind a bookshelf.

"Can I help you?" she asked, peering up beneath a frock of curly silver hair.

"Yes. I'm looking for this book." Emi pulled a small rectangular piece of cardstock out of her purse, and the woman raised her brow as she read the scribble on the back.

"I've been wondering when you would come," she said with a knowing smile.

Emi flipped through the yellow pages of an old book as she strolled back to her car. She felt different, strange, and excited, like something in her that had long been sleeping was beginning to wake.

But she stopped short and watched in awe as a bright little bird with a neon blue coat descended from a tree and landed on the sidewalk directly in front of her. Mesmerized, Emi allowed it to escort her across the street, through an ivy-covered iron gate, and into a little corner park.

The bird led her straight to the middle, beckoning her to sit on one of four curved benches facing a noisy stone fountain. The wind whooshed in the leaves above and fell in a wide spiral around her.

Emi closed her eyes and took a deep breath of autumn air. The gurgling of the water was familiar, but she couldn't quite place it. She reached out and spread her fingers over the bench on either side.

Surprised at what she felt under one of her palms, Emi picked up a thin, frayed band. She turned it over in her fingers, inspecting the black elastic with wonder and awe, and was instantly transported to another place in her mind.

Emi blinked and found herself on the same bench in front of the same fountain, but instead of the corner park, she was in a meadow with wildflowers at her feet, surrounded by a vast green forest. Jesse sat next to her, smiling widely. He reached out his big, warm hands and closed her decades-old hair tie inside hers.

"I'll be waiting for you, Emi Amato, for the rest of my lives."

EPILOGUE

The sun shone so brightly over the Aegean Sea that the waves were too dazzling to look at directly. A few small, white boats bobbed lazily away from the coast in the blue-green waters. The scent of wisteria flowers blew in with the wind, rustling the olive trees, and two purple butterflies with black spots fluttered around the bright pink bougainvillea that framed the mountain overlook. The colorful chalets adorning the bluffs above the water looked so friendly in the afternoon light.

Close to the edge of the vast cliff, an ornate bench sat under an olive tree. And it was here, in the shade, that a young woman sat with an open book. She wore a blue floral dress with buttons down the front, and her dark curls were tucked behind her ears, a few strands falling as her chin dipped. Her brow furrowed thoughtfully as she read, and she was so deep into the pages that she almost didn't hear the interruption.

"Mi scusi, sa che ore sono?"

A young man stood before her. Her olive-shaped eyes met his, dark and familiar, and she understood that they somehow recognized each other. He smiled and removed his hat. She moved over for him to sit.

And she knew, from somewhere deep within, that they had found each other again.

www.ellenestico.com

www.ingramcontent.com/pod-product-compliance
Lightning Source LLC
Chambersburg PA
CBHW030453100526
44580CB00009B/118/J